AMAZON
Complete Expert Guide

The Millionaire's Guide to Selling on Amazon

By Dan Johnson

Published by Media Prestige eBook
Publishing Company

Table of Contents

INTRODUCTION

Guide to millions? Amazon FBA? What is all this you ask?

Let's start off with Amazon. Amazon is an electronic commerce company and is basically the largest internet-based retail company within the United States. It started out as an online bookstore, although, it soon diversified itself to everything from jewelry to video games.

As of the moment there are about two million third-party sellers that are based on the Amazon marketplace worldwide, altogether producing 50% of Amazon's total sales.

Now, if you're a business that sells online and wants to ship, you may want to consider using the Fulfillment by Amazon (FBA) to handle your products for packaging and shipping.

There are a lot of things to cover when you want to use Amazon FBA such as how to setup an account, the fees, and charges, choosing a product, finding a supplier, shipping, after sales, and all those details. This book covers them all from top to bottom! Of course, no matter how long that list of details is, it all ends the same way: **MILLIONS**. With this book, you're sure to achieve that! Make this book your bible. Read it, apply what you learn, and reread it. You'll find more and more information makes perfect sense the second time around.

Are you ready? Are you psyched to earn your first million online? Well, you have the right tool on the palms of your hands. Let's take the next step and cover all the chapters.

CHAPTER 1: WHAT IS FULFILLMENT BY AMAZON (FBA)?

So what is this game-changing way of selling your products you ask?

Amazon has been able to innovate and create one of the most advanced fulfillment networks in the world, with the smart idea of contributing to help other people's businesses in the process.

It's a service that basically has Amazon store the products that you sell in their fulfillment centers. They will be able to do everything from picking, packing and shipping your product with provided customer services.

This has supported so many businesses already, as it helps you scale your business and be able to reach the customers you weren't able to before. A survey was done in 2014 showing that 71% of FBA respondents have reported that their unit sales have increased to 20% more on Amazon.com once they have joined.

This can help your business too.

Let's take this example:

Back in the day, if you wanted to ship items to your customers, you would have to do it one at a time rather than all at once. This meant that as business and sales got better, then you would have to hire employees and more warehouse space. Basically, you'd have a headache.

What Fulfillment by Amazon had done, is that they had taken away all the headache of past problems and provided a simple solution to the problem: *You will ship your products in bulk to Amazon and Amazon will be the ones to pack and ship each individual order that you have received for you*

Isn't that amazing?

That Isn't The Only Benefit Of FBA

But, simply disposing of the headache of shipping isn't any different to all the other fulfillment centers out there that provide the same service Amazon does.

Now you're asking: *What's the big deal with Amazon's fulfillment centers then?*

Well, you don't just have all your products in one place and being shipped for you, but your sales will definitely jump, not just sissy kids jump, but like really a jump when in the use of FBA.

Why Does Sales Increase?

The reason your sales increase when using Amazon's FBA is that now your products can qualify under the Amazon's Free Super Saver Shipping. This basically means that Amazon will be able to offer to your customer free shipping when there is a purchased done over $25

It's not over because Amazon will also be able to offer their Amazon Prime members Free, Two-day shipping on all of your products.

Now, if you think about it, as you are shopping online do you think you would prefer to buy from a seller that is able to offer you a 2-day shipping for Free? People would die for that 2-day Free Shipping. If it weren't there, there would be more of a chance that your customers would just pass on your products. In the end, most of your potential customers would be passing, due to the hassle of adding shipping fee and long shipping time.

Fulfillment by Amazon is able to remove this hurdle along with your headache.

This Business Does Not Sleep

Since Amazon has the responsibility of shipping your products to all your customers, it has to work 24 hours a day in order to make sure that your orders go out fast and can be delivered on time to customers.

You are able to even go on vacation and your business will be able to run on autopilot for you, orders will be able to come in and products will go out as you sip on that Pina Colada.

A Growing Internet Business

Instead of attaining the expensive warehouse space that you need and all the employees you need to hire in order to ship your orders, you are able to work at home and be able to ship your products to Amazon in bulk.

You know what? You can even have any imported goods shipped directly to the Amazon fulfillment centers.

This type of business model allows you to grow rapidly without the need for all the tremendously expensive warehouse space and equipment that would add on to the costs of your business.

You are also able to use this model as a way to manage and ship the orders that your customers have placed in other online markets such as eBay, Buy.com, and others.

What Are The Products That You Are Allowed To Ship To Amazon?

Amazon may have started out as an online outlet for selling books, but it has definitely improved how it was before.

People can now buy jewelry, lawnmowers, beds, electronics and even exercise equipment. You want it; just name it.

You have the ability to ship even media items like books and non-media items like toys, home or garden items and much, much more.

The Fulfillment By Amazon Fees

The Fulfillment by Amazon fees are considerably low, which makes it definitely beneficial for those who have just started out in this business.

The fees may be updated from time to time and change, but the following are what you could expect:

- Fee for Picking (Per Order) = Approximately $1

- Fee for Packing (Per Order) = Approximately $1

- Weight-based Fee (Per Order) = Approximately $0.40 for every pound being shipped to a customer

- Storage Fee = Approximately $0.45 for every cubic foot of storage space that you may need to attain

- Inbound Freight = What it may cost you to ship your products to Amazon

- What's great about inbound freight fee is that Amazon will support you by partnering you up with them on shipping; this means that you will be able to use their shockingly low shipping rates.

All you have to do is to tell Amazon how big and heavy your package will be and the website will produce a label for you to be able to place on your box.

Easy and Simple, don't you think?

To see Amazon FBA's latest fee charges, please check **FBA Fulfillment Fees** page.

- **FBA Fulfillment Fees page:** http://goo.gl/wi1d8g

Does FBA Work Only For People Working From Home?

Of course not!

There are even businesses that have already been in the business of selling online and had already been able to sell thousands upon thousands of products in their online stores even though they weren't using FBA.

After joining the FBA program, their sales and business had increased tremendously.

Is It Possible To Have A Right And A Wrong Way To Use FBA?

Yes, there is.

This is more in the sense that there are strategies that would definitely help your business when using the FBA tactic and there are strategies that would just bring your business down.

Here's an example:

It would be most unfortunate for you and your business if you had decided to purchase vast amounts of products and ship it to the Amazon fulfillment centers just to realize that numerous amounts of other people have already done the same thing you did.

You need to be able to think strategically when you come into this business; you can't just go in blindly.

Ask yourself this: *'What can you and your business provide that no one else has already?'* or *'What can you sell to be unique from all the other businesses?'*

If you want to be able to achieve the different from the usual, then list all the products you have noticed that has not already been in the FBA and you will be able to benefit immensely if you are able to follow this strategy.

Once you take a look at the products that no one else is selling then you are able to sell your products without the worry of the competition within your online market.

Make sure you look for those items that differentiate you from the rest and can be considered desirable to all your potential customers and you will be able to gain so much more sales than you could have ever considered gaining.

a. Reasons To Choose Amazon For Selling

There are numerous other online markets to sell from, Amazon and eBay are two examples. They are both highly successful platforms for selling although they have differences in their operation, shopping experience.

Sellers may get confused as to where and who to go to sell, here's a quick guide as to why choosing Amazon would be most advantageous to your business compared to the rest.

1 - Elegance And Simplicity
Amazon has a very simplistic and organized selling platform in the industry. Comparing Amazon and the other online selling platforms, the others may have a longer process to go through just to get selling.

Amazon's web store interface is also elegant and simple to use which will make your buyer's shopping experience a more enjoyable one.

2 - Attaining Fulfillment Without The Hassle

When using another online market platform, it would be up to you as the seller to see that your buyer gets what they paid for. This basically means that you will either have to create and maintain relationships between fulfillment partner(s) or that you would have to handle your own fulfillment (all the inventory, packaging, and shipping) all on your own.

When in Amazon, you can use their Fulfillment by Amazon, just send everything to Amazon with no cost and let them deal with your headache.

3 - Reduced Overhead

The way Amazon has created its system does not just provide the fulfillment platform, but it allows provides the opportunity to reduce their overhead expenses.

Since, in Amazon, you don't need to produce your own listing or continuously re-list your items on Amazon. Your maintenance overhead levels, as time goes by, will reduce.

The same things happen for the communication time since the buyers and sellers rarely need any communication.

4 - Better Visibility As A Smaller Seller

As a seller that may be just starting out in an online marketing platform, you may be one of those people buried at the end of the search list and covered by all those top-sellers or those that high-level feedbacks due to the innovation of the best match search system.

What Amazon does is that they have created a system that when buyers are searching for an item, the sellers that are shown are rotated. This allows for the new sellers to gain exposure. Since the buyers that go to Amazon, don't technically need to evaluate the sellers then there is almost always guaranteed sale.

5 - Be Where The Industry Has Growth

The online marketplace platform of Amazon has been growing much more rapidly year-by-year than that of any other online marketplace platforms is growing.

So, if you want to be in action then Amazon is for you.

From what this chapter has mentioned, Amazon has a lot to offer than that of any other online marketing platforms.

However, Amazon isn't for everyone; we all have our own dissenting opinions on its operation. But here are just a couple of points that will help you contemplate on the possible advantages you can reap from Amazon.

Amazon isn't Amazon today without the immense marketing and advertising strategies; a pinnacle of technological commerce in the modern era. Amazon is growing in consumers and members each day reaching out to various parts of the globe. One of the apparent benefits of selling on Amazon is the millions of people and markets it is currently attracting. It presents you with open access to sell your products in all five Amazon marketplaces in the safety of your home. There are more chances of you selling your product here than at the local mart. More exposure, more consumers, more money.

It's completely understandable that you're just not used to doing things online and prefer more tangible methods of earning money. However, everyone is using Amazon to expand their business horizons, either surf the wave of revenue or be attached to traditional concepts of business. Amazon is constantly upgrading to keep up with the dynamic world.

It's not to say that you should immediately shut your website or store or any personal retail outside of Amazon; the situation is relative. If your website offers more income to your pockets, then so be it. Nevertheless, Amazon will give you, even more, opportunities on top of your standard income. The idea of it excites you, otherwise, you wouldn't be reading about what you can benefit from Amazon. There's no costly rent in comparison to tangible stores, you don't even need to worry about location. You can save the hassle of marketing your products and have people familiarize your brand. As long as you follow these rules and have the ethical and positive approach to this business, you're good to go.

Perhaps you doubt the faithfulness of the people you transact with; scammers, fraud and all. Have no fear. Amazon's security is something it should boast with novel ways of protecting you and your customers - from strict regulations on timely payments to traceable shipment. Disobedience to the rules will either lower your status to make it difficult to conduct business or ban you completely. Amazon has little tolerance to fraudulent schemes to create a protected working environment for all.

You may think that the added fees on top of your products don't leave you enough room for profit. You may believe that in the end, you'll be the one making a loss. I beg to differ. Amazon has generated components to make it as trouble-free as possible. Features, like the fixed price of the Pro Merchant Subscriptions, actually gives you a heads up on your expenses calculations. The Fulfillment by Amazon (FBA) offers a great deal of ways to increase your sales, customer service available in the local language and Amazon warehouses that stores your products for you. It's a win-win situation.

b. How Does It Work?

Now you have an idea of what Fulfillment by Amazon is and the numerous amounts of benefits that it can provide for you and your business.

How exactly does it work? The way that Fulfillment by Amazon works has been mentioned previously, although, we will now go on an in-depth explanation of how it goes about its process.

In simple words: **Your business sells the items and Amazon ships it**.

Here are steps on how to use the FBA:

> **STEP #1: Send All Your Products To Amazon**
> All of the products from new to used are first sent to Amazon's fulfillment centers.
>
> Here are the sub-steps provided to proceed to send your products to Amazon's fulfillment centers.
>
> - You can do this by first uploading your listings to the Seller Central
>
> - After that, you allow Amazon to fulfill either all or part of your inventory listing
>
> - Print the PDF labeling either provided by Amazon or you can use the Fulfillment by Amazon's label service
>
> - Use the discounted shipping that Amazon provides or you can select your own carrier of choice.

STEP #2: Amazon Will Store All Your Products

Once all your products have been sent to Amazon, they will then catalog your items and store your products in their ready-to-ship inventory

This is how it works:

- Once Amazon has received your products, they will then scan your inventory

- Unit dimensions are then provided to be able to accommodate the storage space needed

- For those who want to monitor their inventory placed in the Amazon's fulfillment center, there is an integrated tracking system established by Amazon.

STEP #3: Customers Will Place Orders For Your Products

Customers who have placed orders directly on Amazon will be fulfilled by Amazon.

- Your listings on Amazon will be ranked by the prices presented with no shipping costs added since those items are entitled to free shipping for purchases that are over $35*.

- For those customers on Amazon Prime*, they can upgrade their shipping options in order to eligible FBA listings.

* This excludes multi-channel fulfillment orders that have been placed on other websites and services that include Amazon Webstore or the Checkout by Amazon.

STEP #4: Amazon Will Be The Ones To Pick And Pack Your Products

The products for sale that have been ordered by customers will be picked and packaged for delivery

This is how it works:
- Amazon will be the one to locate your products through the use of advanced web-to-warehouse, high-speed picking and a sorting system that Amazon has developed

- Customers are allowed to combine different ordered with other products that have been fulfilled by Amazon

STEP #5: Amazon Then Ships Your Products To The Customers

Amazon will then be able to ship the products the customers have requested through their network of fulfillment centers

This is how it works:

- Amazon will choose whichever method is comfortable for them for shipping

- Tracking information is provided for the customers

- For orders placed on Amazon.com, customers are able to contact customer's services for any inquiries.

YouTube Video Tutorials
- **How Fulfillment by Amazon (FBA) works:** https://goo.gl/cRWhEE
- **Tour of Fulfillment by Amazon (FBA):** https://goo.gl/1D6usZ
- **How Amazon Receives Your Inventory:** https://goo.gl/CAAYgH
- **Amazon FBA - What It Is And How it Works!:** https://goo.gl/smjfN8
- **How to Start an Online Business on Amazon the RIGHT way with no Technical Knowledge:** https://goo.gl/R8xBZu

c. Why Is FBA a Big Deal?

With all the big buzz of Fulfillment by Amazon, some sellers may be wondering: FBA is just another fulfillment method, isn't it? What's all this talk about the use of FBA? Basically, **What's the big deal about FBA?**

FBA becomes a big deal once you realize the amount of support it can place on your online business. For some, it becomes a **major decision** in their business in terms of profit that they will be making during their online career.

Those who may get to feel the best effect of the FBA are those who are small business owners, these people may not have the most efficient fulfillment systems in their arsenal and may not want to risk any potential negative effects from a poor customer experience.

Although there is plenty amounts of benefits that a seller can gain from using FBA, you should also never forget the following:

- Not every third-party seller should use FBA; it all really depends on the individual seller's financial resources as well as the nature of his or her business.

- Sellers should look at FBA as another weapon in their arsenal and not as a blanket resource. Sellers should either be 100% FBA or 100% FBM (Fulfillment by Merchant), although most professional sellers have become a hybrid of both

- Not all the products that have been submitted for FBA will end up being a good candidate for a number of reasons, mainly size, performance of their sales and their margin.

d. How FBA affects Product Discoverability and Buyability?

Before we get into learning on how FBA affects product Discoverability and Buyability, we will first look into the two terms:

1. Discoverability

This is the ability for your product listing to be found on Amazon. Amazon focuses on the type of search results on the different products rather than the type of seller

When it comes to having people be able to reach your products, FBA products are indeed the ones who get more discoverable for two reasons:

Reason #1: Amazon Prime Members

Prime members are those who spend more time shopping on Amazon than the average customer.

These customers are entitled to filtering out all the non-Prime offers, which basically takes away those products that aren't in the FBA listing system.

Reason #2: Amazon's Reputation

Even if your product does by chance show up on the shoppers list, there will be items that will possess the offer that shows *'Fulfillment by Amazon'* and are more desirable for customers due to the efficient and traceable delivery process

2. Buyability

A product's likelihood of being bought or in more actionable terms, this is the product's chance of winning the Buy Box

Here are the effects on Buyability:

Reason #1: Seller's Rating

FBA sellers will not gain any negative ratings on the metrics of On-Time Delivery Rate and Late Shipment Rate due to FBA.

Reason #2: Fulfillment Latency

FBA items are instantly placed in the shortest latency windows, while FBM offers might proceed to be in longer windows (ex. 3-4 business days)

e. Advantages of Amazon FBA

Using Fulfillment by Amazon offers huge benefits for sellers like you. Here are the best benefits you can get by using Amazon FBA:

1- Accessibility to the Prime Members

As an online seller, you couldn't ask for a better customer. These Prime Members subscribe at least $99 a year in order to take full advantage of the free shipping that Amazon has to offer.

These Prime Members are not only loyal customers, but they are the ones who tend to purchase items that are more expensive and buy at least %150 more than any of the non-Prime Members. To see these in number basis, they spend around $1,340 on Amazon annually, while non-Prime Members spend only around %529

The use of FBA allows for a wider customer base. There is a speculation of around 50 million Prime Member subscribers in Amazon right now. If you think about, that's a lot of money.

2 - The Care for Shipping, Returns, and Customer Service

Amazon handles everything from picking the item, packing it and shipping it to your customers.

Quick and swift shipping gives you happy customers and with happy customers provides with increased sales.

Amazon will also be able to handle any of the unsatisfied customers. This will definitely save the time and money for you because you won't need to employ any additional customer service reps.

Since your items will be stored in Amazon's fulfillment centers, you won't need to gain the headache of where to get the space to fit your inventory.

3 - Buy Box Win

Those in FBA, depending on the category of the product, can place its price at least 10 – 20% higher than the average competitor and still be able to win the Buy Box. That is if you are using FBA and your competitors are not.

This is because shipping is added into the cost. If your items are priced at $20 with a Prime Member shipping, it will beat out a merchant item of $15 with $5 shipping.

4 - Increased Volume of Sales

This may not be a guarantee, but it has been found that those who switch over recognize a rise in unit sales volume to about 20% more. Numerous amounts of sellers have reported higher or even double of their original volume. This is mainly due to the Prime Member subscribers.

5 - Customers are Inclined to Pay More for the Same Product

The millions of Prime Member subscribers on Amazon will know a great deal when they see it. As mentioned in one of the benefits, sellers who are in FBA could factor in the cost of shipping into the price. Some Prime Members are willing to pay a few more bucks to be able to ensure that the delivery is prompted in two days and the added convenience.

6 - No Such Thing as an Inventory Limit

Since Amazon does your inventory for you, you can sell as much as you want without the worry of the amount of storage requirements that you need. Amazon possesses one of the most advanced fulfillment networks in the whole world that will allow you, as a seller, to store as much products as you please with the use of their automated inventory tracker. Your products are guaranteed safety.

YouTube Video Tutorials
- **Amazon FBA: 3 Benefits to Selling on Amazon FBA:** https://goo.gl/LqpiWG
- **Pros and Cons of Selling on Amazon: https://goo.gl/ecmWV9**
- **Amazon FBA Canada: Pros & Cons of FBA Canada:** https://goo.gl/n5SFra

f. Disadvantages of Amazon FBA

Like any other business, Amazon FBA also comes with some disadvantages that a seller has to deal with. Here are some Amazon FBA disadvantages you should take in mind:

1 - Not All Products Sold are Profitable with FBA

The products that have a low volume and low margins are the ones that will end up not being profitable to sell with the use of FBA. Furthermore, any items that are heavy and inexpensive low margin items that may require for you to have higher storage fees may be the items that blow out your profits.

2 - Amazon Will Not Be Able to Ship Certain Items

Some items that may be deemed as hazardous are severely prohibited and these items will not be shipped by the Amazon's fulfillment centers. Examples of these items include: any type of flammable liquids, flammable solids, and aerosols. Some beauty products may fall under this category.

3 - Fees, Glorious Fees

FBA may seem like a miracle service, although there are some pitfalls with its use.

The biggest one among many of its pitfalls is the numerous amounts of fees associated with FBA.

To start, sellers on Amazon are required to either have a Pro Merchant ($39.95/month) account or the Advantage account ($29.95/year), which have different limitations to what a seller can and cannot do.

Next, FBA charges a certain amount for storage fee for the items that are unsold in Amazon's fulfillment centers. When your items don't sell, FBA customers are charged at rates that can vary from $0.40/cubic foot per month to $0.60 cubic foot per month.

Overall, depending on the type of online business that you are in, you might want to proceed with FBA or not. Take your time to think about it because if it is good for your business it can go far, although if it is not it may destroy what you built.

YouTube Video Tutorials
- **Part 1: What Is FBA? - The Introduction:**
  https://goo.gl/rJCghN
- **Part 2: Signing up for FBA & Sourcing:**
  https://goo.gl/dFPMmc
- **Part 3: Organizing and Listing Inventory:**
  https://goo.gl/VSEpVH
- **Part 4: Rules, Guidelines, and Supplies:**
  https://goo.gl/QnvW9v

- **Part 5: Packaging Your First Shipment:** https://goo.gl/Wh2uCW , **How to Package Items For Amazon FBA - Save Money & Clear Up Misconceptions:** https://goo.gl/QyZGG6
- **Part 6: Finalizing Your First Shipment:** https://goo.gl/e6ypDK
- **All Parts: The Complete Series:** https://goo.gl/vp8sK2

CHAPTER 2: HOW TO REGISTER?

Selling on the internet is the best way to give your business a productivity boost. In this era where people make a lot of their shopping online, it is almost a necessity. However, setting up an online shop can be complicated and expensive.

Using Amazon FBA makes this a lot easier, and anyone who reads this book can create an online shop. However, if you want to do it right, it is important you do it right from the beginning.

These are the steps to register as an amazon seller, follow them to make sure you give your new internet business a great start!

To begin with the Amazon FBA registration process, look for the "**sell**" link in the amazon homepage or log on directly to **Amazon Services Seller Central** site and do the self-registration process. Choose from the two seller type: Individual or Professional.

Sell Link: http://goo.gl/jWFiue

Amazon Services Seller Central site: http://goo.gl/K8iyyz

Individual vs. Professional

There are two types of Amazon seller accounts. They are called individual and professional. The first thing you will be asked to do while registering is choosing one of these two plans.

While you can change between the two without much work, it is better if you choose the right one from the start. Think carefully about the kind of business you want (or already have) and consider the benefits of each one of these plans.

1 - Individual:

This is Amazon basic seller plan and it has no registration or maintenance fees. When you sell as an individual, every sell you make has a 0.99$ fee. You should choose this on if you only have a few items and you don't plan to sell in bulk.

2 - Professional:

This is amazon premium seller's plan and it has a monthly fee of 39.99$. Now, this may sound like a lot, but if you are selling too many products with an individual plan then the 0.99$ fee adds up really fast. As a professional, you won't have this fee.

There are other benefits to this plan. For example, a professional can sell items of any categories. Things like clothes and media are closed to individual sellers and only professionals can sell them.

Do note that you can easily upgrade from an individual to a professional account. If you are not sure of the kind of results you will get, it is wise to open and individual account and upgrade when you start selling a lot.

a. Four Steps in Amazon FBA Registration

STEP #1: Basic Information

After you choose the type of account you will open, it is time to enter your information. This happens automatically if you already have an Amazon account.

If that is not the case, then you will have to enter basic information like your name, address and phone number.

It is highly recommended that in this section you take a moment to read the terms and conditions that apply to Amazon seller's accounts. This is extremely important because by reading these documents you will understand your rights and where you stand if any problems arise. Also, there are a lot of Amazon policies that will apply to your sales and you need to keep them in mind.

STEP #2: Billing Information

After you are done with the basic information, you will be asked to fill out a form with your "charge information". In this step, Amazon will ask for a valid credit or debit card information, as well as a billing address. They will use this information to charge you for any fees that their services may generate. You can skip these steps and finish it later, but if you have the info at hand there is no reason to delay it any further.

STEP #3: Contact Information

The third step is the one where you will give Amazon your business and contact information. First you will need to tell amazon if you are a private person or a registered business. Make sure you make the right choice here, as you can't change this information later on.

If you are a registered business, you will be asked to provide a little extra info. Make sure you put the right information at this point, since this information will have legal implications later on. It is important that you keep your contact information updated, since is the one Amazon will use to get in contact with you should any problems arise.

STEP #3: Phone Verification

The last step is the phone verification. Amazon will call you if you gave them a landline number or send a text if you provided a mobile number. After the verification, you will land at a confirmation, where you will be shown all the info you provided. Now you can start enjoying all the benefits an Amazon account gives you.

YouTube Video Tutorials

- **How to Set Up Your Amazon FBA Seller Account:** https://goo.gl/DyZLXQ
- **Quick 3 Minute Set Up Of Your Seller Central Account:** https://goo.gl/A1NQtF
- **How To Get Started Selling A Product On Amazon Setting Up Your Account & Product Listing:** https://goo.gl/MJWCM4

b. Setting Up Your Seller Central Account

The Amazon seller central is the single most powerful tool at your disposal when you are a merchant on Amazon. But there are a lot of people who don't really know it, they don't learn about it and never use it to its full potential.

If you want to be a successful seller on Amazon, then you need to learn all the techniques and tricks that come with this tool so you can use it efficiently. There are a lot of things you can do on this place, but we will highlight the most important ones.

1 - Order Management

When you start to sell a lot on Amazon, chances are you will start getting a little overwhelmed with the amounts of orders you can receive. Luckily, the seller central has a great tool to keep all these orders organized. Get used to checking this feature at least once every day so you can get every order delivered on time.

Also, this feature makes it easy to cancel or refund orders, and even print text reports if you want to keep everything in your hands or give your customers a physical report of their orders.

2 - Customization

The seller central lets you set up almost anything on your account. You can customize the policies that apply to your items, putting your own logo or explain your refund policies to the customers. But these are just the simplest of features; the seller central can go even deeper to give your internet business a boost.

Setting up discounts and promotions to be shown during your customer's checkout. Determining your own shipping rates, integrating the Amazon checkout system in your own website. There are a lot of tools to make your business successful. Use them!

3 - Setting Up Your Account For FBA

The FBA (Fulfilled By Amazon) service is a premium service that Amazon offers its merchants. It gives you the opportunity to ship your products in bulk to Amazon warehouses where they will handle all the shipping process. This means you can sit back and relax while Amazon handles all the order processing and product delivery.

Of course, this has many advantages, but the main one is that your products can be eligible for Free shipping and the two-day shipping service that Amazon offers its prime users. Most customers will look for free shipping in everything they buy, and it can be a selling point for many persons.

This service makes it a lot more likely that people will buy your products since you are now backed by Amazon delivery policies and every product that is fulfilled by Amazon has extra visibility on the search results page.

The first thing you need to do is to register your account for FBA. You can do this by clicking on "get started" on the FBA main page. After you have your account set up you can start setting products to the Amazon warehouses, but first you need to set them up for shipping on your inventory.

In your seller central, you need to go to your inventory and select the products you want to add to your FBA listing. In the actions tab, select "change to Fulfilled by amazon". This way, your products will start enjoying the benefits of being fulfilled by Amazon.

After this is done, make sure you pack your products nicely to avoid any delays in the FBA cycle. In you seller central you can print amazon labels that you have to put on any product you intend to ship to the warehouse.

YouTube Video Tutorials
- **Seller Central Tutorial - Account Settings:** https://goo.gl/mcKUAe
- **Amazon Seller Central Settings:** https://goo.gl/bDXpnJ

c. Differences Between Amazon and eBay

Whether you are an established eBay seller thinking about expanding or making the switch to Amazon, or just someone who is trying to choose between the two to start their internet business. There are many key differences between the services that you need to understand before making a decision.

One of these differences and maybe the most important is the orientation of the site. Amazon is a lot more "buyer oriented", where everything it's geared towards inviting people to buy directly from them and making it easy to browse and find a lot of different products. EBay on the other hand is a lot more seller-oriented, encouraging buyers to sell their products on the store.

1 - Goodbye Auctions

If you already have an established business on eBay, then this will be the first and most shocking difference between the two services. Auction style selling is extremely important on eBay, but on Amazon it just doesn't exist,

If you use this eBay feature extensively, then you will need to really evaluate how to get into Amazon and understand that things will work very differently for you in the new service.

2 - Easy listing

Another main difference is how much faster is to create a listing for an item in Amazon compared to eBay. When putting a new product of yours for sale, you won't have to spend a lot of time putting new information, writing a flashy description or uploading pictures.

You just have to find the product on the Amazon catalog, list yourself as a seller and set your price. It is also a lot less time consuming to maintain your listings on Amazon. Unlike eBay, where you have to constantly relist products if they don't sell, you don't really need to do anything from the moment you create the listing till the day of the sale.

3 - Strict Policies

If you are used to the freedom that exists on eBay then it may take some time getting used to selling on Amazon. There are a lot of Key policies that are handled by Amazon and you must adhere to them if you want to keep selling there.

Amazon has a 30-day return policy for most items, and shipping time options that you must respect. Amazon also handles checkout and payment processes and there are no other options. This, of course, has the advantage of saving you time, as you won't have a lot of configuration to do.

4 - Customer Comes First

On Amazon, customer service and experience is one of the top priorities. They want to be recognized as a customer focused company and if you want to have a good rank it is extremely important that you follow this philosophy. Unlike eBay, you are a lot more entwined with Amazon as a company and they want you to represent their values.

This means that while selling on eBay can be relatively "hands-off" and relaxed, selling on Amazon will require a lot more work and you will need to use their features and tools often. This won't make it harder though, as Amazon wants a pleasant experience for their sellers too and their tools are built for this.

5 - Fulfilled by Amazon

Amazon goes a long way, making your seller life as easy as possible. This is seen in their features and tools, and it reaches its maximum expression in the FBA program. Amazon offers you the possibility of putting a lot of your business, like shipping, storage and checkout in their hands. Giving you more time to enjoy the benefits and saving you a lot of the headaches that may exist in a big business. There's nothing quite like this on eBay.

YouTube Video Tutorials

- **eBay vs Amazon FBA (Fulfilled By Amazon) - Comparison:** https://goo.gl/UllrEC
- **Amazon FBA vs eBay, "New" Condition:** https://goo.gl/f2iEnu

CHAPTER 3: IDENTIFYING PRODUCTS TO SELL

When it comes to selling products, we need to find a single good and profitable product rather than looking for a market to operate in. Instead of limiting yourself to a single market and searching for a product to sell within it, we should do it the other way around and find a product that is known to be good and then find a market for it. If your goal is solely to make income and not branch out into new products then, this is the way to do it.

a. Steps How to Find Good Products

Follow these steps to find good products to sell on Amazon FBA:

1 - Check the Amazon Best-Sellers

Begin by checking out the Amazon.com Best Sellers: The hottest products on Amazon. Select 3 different categories that interest you. From the 3 categories, you can select 1 category to focus on, for the mean time, while you are still starting. You can also work with the other 2 categories later on when you are already familiar with how Amazon FBA works. Getting interested in your selected category will help your selling on FBA more fun and easier.

2 - Find Products with Good Reviews and Less Sellers

Search for products with excellent reviews but few sellers. Usually, these products are not the top sellers in your selected category but this will help you achieve the power to be competitive with other sellers on FBA.

When selling on Amazon FBA, you need to know the differences between a good product and a bad one in order to properly choose what to sell. So, let's start with what makes a product good and profitable.

YouTube Video Tutorials
- **Amazon Private Label Product Research Process:** https://goo.gl/K99BPH
- **Product Research for Amazon FBA Private Label:** https://goo.gl/aN8Xs6
- **How To Find A Profitable Product To Sell On Amazon (Step-By-Step Tutorial):** https://goo.gl/rPW44a
- **Criteria For Picking Profitable Products To Sell & Private Label On Amazon:** https://goo.gl/yZC27L
- **How to Find the Best Products to Sell on Amazon & Find High Quality, Low Cost Suppliers:** https://goo.gl/C4KHUR
- **How to use Sales Rank to Find Products to Sell on Amazon.com:** https://goo.gl/QKrGvn

b. Good Products

Follow Your Passion is definitely the most horrible advice you could possibly give or get – particularly with regards to selecting a product to sell online. If a flourishing online business is your ultimate goal, it is best to use a systematic strategy and select a niche with characteristics favorable to online success.

Here are 6 different ways to help you discover a niche as well as products to sell.

1. Accessory-Heavy Niche categories:

Accessories can have markups as high as 100 to 1000%, and buyers are noticeably less price tag conscious regarding these products. A customer might go shopping for several weeks to obtain the best price for a TV, and yet wouldn't hesitate about wasting $30 on an HDMI wire cable. However, there's a great possibility the business endeavor produced quite as much earnings on the HDMI cable as it would do on the flat TV screen. If you select a niche with plenty of accessories, you'll have the benefit of substantially bigger income margins and lesser price tag-sensitive buyers.

2. Buyers with Great Passion or Problem:

It's surprising the amounts of money enthusiastic hobbyists are willing to pay. Mountain bikers can spend hundreds of dollars on small accessories to get rid of extra weight, and passionate fishermen are likely to spend thousands upon thousands of dollars in sailboats and associated gadgets. Also, if you are able to provide a product-based method for fixing a really painful problem, you will get a target market desperate to actually buy the products you are selling.

3. Products over $10 to $200:

Your selling price should be over $10 and under $200. There's much room for profit within these ranges.

Products under $10 will not give sufficient profit after shipping and fees while products over $200 are too pricey for users and they will put much thought and time into purchasing which will in return affect your profits.

I've discovered that this budget range is a "sweet spot" for online stores. It's big enough to sufficiently generate good income, yet small enough that – with an excellent and informative description – the majority of buyers won't have to personally talk to the vendor before the purchase.

However if you sell items that price $500 and higher, a large number of shoppers will require customer support service before buying.

4. Difficult to Get Locally:
When you need garden tools, you'd probably go to your nearest Hardware Store. But where could you check out to purchase video surveillance devices or magicians' equipment? Most likely on the internet. Choose specialized niche products which are difficult to get at local stores, and you will be in time to find yourself in front of a large number of your potential customers while they search the internet.

Although you preferably choose a product hard to source in your area, likewise you have to make sure there's enough demand for this product! This may be a fine line to distinguish.

5. Slow Upgrade Products:

If your product offering is always changing every year, you'll find yourself investing precious time in resources which will soon be out-of-date. Choose products that don't go out-of-date easily.

6. Disposable and Consumable Products:

Returning clients are very important to every online store, and it's definitely a lot easier to sell your products to your present clients who have confidence in you compared to new potential customers. In cases where your products need to be re-supplied regularly – and you think you can keep your clients satisfied – then you are on the right track to creating a lucrative business with continuous earnings.

7. Specific Niche Products:

Good products are usually specific products. What I mean is you will not be selling "bracelets" but specifically "Silver Eagle Charm Bracelets". In this way, you can put all your focus on one single item and not be confused juggling around different products. We also want our products to be small and light. This way it can be easily packaged and shipped at a lower cost, maximizing your profits.

8. Continuous Streams of customers:

Your products also need a consistent flow of buyers that will purchase your product all year long.

This means, don't try to sell products that will be obsolete within the year, an example would be iPhone 5 cases when the iPhone 6 has been out on the market. Also, avoid seasonal products such as Halloween decorations or Christmas lights.

9. Small and light-weight Products:
The larger and heavier the product, the more expensive it will cost you to ship to Amazon. Products with weight from 2-3 pounds and below are preferable.

10. 100% Markup Products
Selling for two times more than your purchase price – These kinds of products are highly preferred but sometimes hard to find. Which means, if I can't sell it two times the price, I'm not selling it on Amazon FBA as a long term product.

c. Bad Products

If there are good products to sell, there are bad products too. These are the products that I wouldn't sell on Amazon FBA:

1. Mechanical Products:
Anything mechanical or have high-quality standards are going to be very stressful to deal with.

Products such as hydraulic machines, factory and construction types of machinery, will be very difficult to purchase, store and ship after you make you a sale. It's much easier to stay with simple products. The same applies to products that are fragile and require very delicate packaging.

2. Power seller Products:

Any product that other companies are already selling in high volume. Do not believe that you will be able to sell boxer briefs when you have 15 other companies on Amazon selling 20,000 units a month straight from the factory. You will not be able to compete. In order to find a profitable product we need to find one that is always selling but do not have many sellers.

3. Trademarked Products

If you sell Trademarked products, chances are, you might be sued and get out of business very fast. This applies to counterfeit products such as purses and watches.

4. Fragile Products:

These products demand best delivery procedures – It's not just a major problem, but a torture waiting for you.

YouTube Video Tutorials

- **Amazon FBA Clearance Arbitrage Trip - Making Money Shopping at WalMart:** https://goo.gl/RKoBTi
- **Retail Arbitrage: Making money in your Amazon FBA and Ebay business:** https://goo.gl/0mlU0u
- **The Best Three Product Categories To Sell On AMAZON FBA:** https://goo.gl/7c55uH

- **10 Items That Sell On Amazon FBA That You Have Passed Up:** https://goo.gl/m9EBFV
- **5 More Items to Flip on Amazon FBA:** https://goo.gl/ZAGnYX
- **The Top 5 Item Types That Sell Well On Amazon:** https://goo.gl/TGecVV

CHAPTER 4: FINDING PRODUCT SUPPLIERS

Choosing the right products to sell could be overwhelming. Go over this chapter for the guidelines on how to look for potential products to sell. These references will give you information which marketplace to look for a product to sell online, the number of competitors and the right prices to sell.

There are 3 major ways how you can source your products to sell. In this section, I will discuss them briefly:

YouTube Tutorials
- **Easiest Items to Sell on Amazon for a Profit:**
  https://goo.gl/3yb6QX

- **How To Find Wholesale Suppliers & Manufacturers To Private Label A Product And Sell On Amazon:** https://goo.gl/gxhekJ
- **Selling on Amazon For Beginners - Finding Suppliers To Private Label Your Product:** https://goo.gl/CZhUAx

---

a. Sourcing from Online Wholesale Stores

With this method, you buy existing products from online stores that sell products cheaper on wholesale.

These will be step by step the process how to source your products from an online wholesale store:

- Select an online wholesaler with good reviews and best price.

- Test the supplier by buying, at least, one piece of the product as an example.

- Buy a dozen pieces if you like the quality of the product.

- List your products on Amazon FBA

- Pack, Label, and Send your products to Amazon FBA warehouse.

- **Advanced Step:** Ask the supplier if they dropship to Amazon FBA. Many wholesale suppliers dropship to Amazon, but you have to be very careful. When you already trust them, you can have them dropship your products to Amazon directly. This is a risk you have to take if you want your online business fully automated.

Suppliers are very important to almost all online businesses. Without suppliers to supply you with products to resell, you will find a difficult time expanding your online business.

Here are just a few online stores where you can source your products for Amazon FBA:

- www.alibaba.com
- www.salehoo.com
- www.dhgate.com
- www.busytrade.com
- www.barncatmercantile.com
- www.powersalez.com
- www.1stopwholesale.com
- www.enricoproducts.com
- www.bdkauto.com
- www.nextsuccess.com
- www.4blackpaws.com
- www.wholesalecrafts.com
- www.serenityteasips.com

- www.snowonder.com
- www.cornellgifts.com
- www.motorcycleleatherstore.com
- www.reikowireless.com
- www.designtimewatch.com
- www.whimsicalwatches.com
- www.desden.com
- www.santafestoneworks.com
- www.atimportsltd.com
- www.station1wholesale.com
- www.outdooractivegear.com

These are just a few of the online stores available on the web. Research from these sites and look at the market data to have a comparison between Alibaba and the rest of the online retailer sites. As you go along, you'll gain opportunities from several venues of finding the good product. Just remember the criteria of a good product when you do the research.

The data you get from these sites can be listed on a spreadsheet to make a summary and track the different products you'll find. You can check a **sample spreadsheet** which is advisable to do from Will Mitchell, a serial entrepreneur.

Get the markup estimate of each product you'll find especially if a product fits all the criteria of a good product. Go over your list as you calculate the selling price of a product.

Honestly, there could be no fixed process in doing a research on a good product. But, there are several ideas that you can try to come up with products to search such as:

- Products that are best-sellers on Amazon

- Products that have been trending in recent years

- Random objects around

- Products people buy consistently with impulse

- Products from random search results

- Randomly clicking the online retail sites (Alibaba, DHgate, etc.)

Researching may take you less than half an hour to find a product. Remember to look for specific products by going through each product subcategories you're searching. Try to list few products on your spreadsheet. Afterwards, check each product again and make a comparison. Make sure to double check and review according to the criteria so you'll avoid having a bad product on your list.

YouTube Video Tutorials
- **Starting An Amazon FBA Business - The Complete Series:** https://goo.gl/GQefTQ

- **Signing up for FBA & Sourcing:**
  https://goo.gl/GX2KAw
- **Amazon FBA Retail Arbitrage and More:**
  https://goo.gl/Skh3ac
- **Amazon Haul Video and Breakdown:**
  https://goo.gl/Up89Yk

b. Sourcing from Local Product Sources

Sometimes, sourcing products from local sources can also be a good option. The reason being is, you can right away see the quality of the product before buying it. And once you bought it, you can send it right away to Amazon FBA warehouse.

Here are some local product sources where you can find a good product to sell on Amazon FBA:

1 - Garage Sale

Most sellers start their inventory from home or garage sales because it opens great opportunities to make huge profits on inventory-- turning 100-1000% profit. There are varieties of products from garage sales that are cheap and you can sell online for a higher price.

To source from garage sales, select a few areas that you're interested in visiting or check the newspaper for some information on upcoming garage sales. Make sure to always start early when scouting items in garage sales to make sure that you'll get the best deal early on.

2 - Thrift Stores

Sourcing items from thrift stores is a practical choice especially for sellers with a limited amount of capital to put up a large inventory. Looking for items in thrift stores does not mean looking for junk; you can find some new items and be able to sell them for big profits. You can also consider buying some used items at thrift stores and still profit from it.

You have the advantage of selling items from thrift stores because you'll have minimal competition from other sellers aside from the very high profits you can make from these items. Just ensure that price stickers are removed and items are cleaned up before shipping to Amazon.

3 – Local Factories & Outlets

If your area is near a factory or factory outlets, you could source your products cheaply. All you need to do is to search your telephone directory or search Google for product factories near your area.

Factories usually sell products on a factory price with a small minimum order.

As you start your relationship with them, you can easily re-order items that sell more. And if the relationship with them prospers, you may ask for exclusivity to sell on Amazon. More so, different products can be tied up from these factory sources and come up with your own packages and make a unique product.

On your journey to selling on Amazon, you'll be an expert in finding a good product sooner or later. Expertise also comes as you continue to get familiar with the line of products you're listing, so you can better serve the needs of the customers.

1. How to Find Good Factory & Outlet Suppliers?

Here's a step-by-step process in finding factory suppliers:

STEP #1: Establish Trust

First, contact your local product factory. Find their contact number or email address if they have posted it online. When talking to them be sure to talk in a professional manner. State your company and the products you are interested in. Ask for their product brochures if they have a digital file and have them send it to your email address.

When using an email address for business, use a professional sounding email (such as: jbc_products@outlook.com, not: sexygirl_4u@yahoo.com).

Remember, when you contact a local factory in your area, see yourself as a big business entity even though you are a newbie. You have to show good impression whenever you talk to their personnel, as this will build their trust to you as an online company.

Know the language in their product niche; show them that you are well informed about the kinds of products they are selling.

STEP #2: Determine What You Are Looking For

Second, after seeing the product brochure and initial contact, you need to determine which specific product you are interested in purchasing. Visit their nearest factory outlet to see the product in person. When you like the quality of their product, ask them if they have a minimum purchase order for the specific product you are interested in selling on Amazon FBA.

This would allow you to order bulk pieces at the source of production at a low cost resulting to a higher profit margin. However, it is preferable for you to start small to get used to the business, build trust with your factory suppliers and it would also prevent you from having a big loss if ever the products don't click.

STEP #3: Make A Deal

Third, try striking a deal with the factory manufacturers. After comparing their factory price and the Amazon FBA prices online, if you think you can make a huge margin on their products, you should ask them if they can customize the product, for example, the color and materials used. You can even ask them to customize the logo and use your brand logo. If they don't customize, you can buy the product as is.

You can also talk to them about drop shipping:

- Many factories now dropship to Amazon. If they do dropship to Amazon FBA, perfect. This is very helpful, as you won't need to worry about space storage.

- If they don't dropship, then you just purchase their products and ship them to Amazon.

2. How to Work with Factory Suppliers?

Online sellers often make the mistake of assuming that once you've sealed a deal with a factory supplier, everything is done. However, the challenging part of this process is not to find a good factory supplier, but actually maintaining a strong and beneficial partnership. Here are a few tips on how to accomplish this venture:

1 - Communication

The continuous dialogue will further strengthen the bond between you and your factory supplier. If you have a problem, bring up the issue with courtesy and respect. The aim is to overcome the obstacle and reach a compromise instead of worsening the issue with emotional attachments.

2 - Equal Bargain Negotiation

Just like in any business environment, you'll need to put yourself in your supplier's perspective. Think like a supplier. You are in this negotiation to achieve financial gain. As a client, you cannot expect to pitch a proposal that would provide an inconvenience to the supplier. With that in mind, when compromising on the terms, provide a win-win situation by understanding the supplier's reservations and position.

Another side tip would be to deposit around 50-70% to your orders beforehand, this allows you to have a higher settlement power since almost, if not, all of the time suppliers are only concerned about getting paid. This deposit proves your adherence to your work.

3 - Learn The Language

You'll need to be able to converse fluently using the terminology of the trade. You'll be more competent boosting your reliability and commitment to making the business deal work. There's nothing more disappointing than an associate who don't know what they're doing.

4 - Be Reliable

This part actually is all about time management and respectful behavior. When you set a date and time with the supplier, you have to be there early or on time. Being late is an insult to any business meetings. When you promise to pay a certain amount of money, be sure you have to follow it through. In order to make a long-term and profitable relationship work, don't make a promise when you know you'll end up not fulfilling it.

5 - Show Your Options

When negotiating, show that you're committed to getting the agreement work, but if things don't turn out in your favor, have the confidence to walk away. Have a backup plan if ever you reach a stalemate with neither of the parties surrendering. This, in turn, would prevent you from agreeing to a contract based on pressure and desperateness.

It's more desirable if you've found a satisfactory relationship with a factory supplier who has a positive outlook, a supplier who shares the same morals and vision as you do. If you've followed each point on "How to Work Factory Suppliers" religiously, but the supplier creates a hostile working environment, I suggest you cease the partnership and find another company. It's not you, it's them. Don't be hesitant to leave because, in the long run, negative conduct will gravely affect the business and your profit, plus adding further stress on your part.

c. Sourcing from Private Label Manufacturers

The best sources of Amazon FBA products are the white label or private label manufacturers.

A private label product is a physical product manufactured by a manufacturing company (the supplier) that other businesses (the seller) can put their own branding to create the impression as though they themselves created the product.

Private label products are often called store brands, white label brands, private brands, house brands, own brands, own label brands, retailer brands and sometimes generic brands. These brands often have the same quality of the well-known brands since many well-known branded products were also created through a private label manufacturer.

If ever you really want to grow your online selling business, you need to create and grow your own brand through private label. By going through this route, you will be able to build a brand with different products under it that you can sell. By creating your own brand, your existing customers who really love your products will turn into loyal and continuous buyers that will generate a steady passive monthly income for you.

The downside of this sourcing route is: it will take longer time and more money than the other product sources. However, the rewards are greater.

YouTube Video Tutorials
- **How To Research And Find Products To Private Label On Amazon:** https://goo.gl/amrFxv
- **Private Label Product Research For Amazon FBA Sellers:** https://goo.gl/Gzd5NS
- **How to Get Started as an Amazon FBA Private Label Seller - 10 Simple Steps:** https://goo.gl/NFVXVZ
- **How to Build a Successful Amazon Private Label Seller Business this Year and Beyond:** https://goo.gl/yaaNJ7
- **Should you Customize Your First Private Label Product?:** https://goo.gl/IWuCA7
- **Getting Started with Private Labeling and Amazon FBA: $33k in 30 Days?:** https://goo.gl/DWPZeu
- **The Private Labeling Amazon Millionaire: Interview:** https://goo.gl/MUXZQP

1. How to Produce Private Label Products

To begin with the private label sourcing, you need to create a product that will look special and unique, that will really stand out from other brands of the same type.

The Internet has made everything possible for online businesses. You don't need any more to go to China and find the best factory to manufacture your products to sell online.

Now, all of your communications can be done through Skype chat or email even at the comforts of your home.

Here are the steps to follow when you decide to create your own Private Label Products:

Step #1: Search for OEM manufacturers

The first step is to contact several manufacturers which have a good track record of producing high-quality products. Searching and connecting with them is really much easier than you might think.

You go over to **Alibaba.com**, searched for "[type of product] OEM", for example, "hand bag OEM". Alibaba is an online store for wholesale products. In there, you could find contact details of factories in China. OEM stands for "Original Equipment Manufacturer", this means that they are willing to manufacture products for other companies.

Step #2: Email OEM manufacturers

Look through all the search results and email the several manufacturers that you like. Explain to them briefly, what you want your product to look like. At this point of time, should be able to show them a drawing of how your product would look like. Once everything is settled, ask them to send you some sample products.

Step #3: Choose the best manufacturer

When the sample products arrive from the different manufacturers, choose the best factory that you think has created the best quality product.

Step #4: Test the product and create some improvements

Test the prototype product if it works well for daily use. Look through the materials, colors, and even logo branding. If there are materials used that look cheap, ask the manufacturer for a specific change. By using more expensive materials, the producing cost will become higher. But if you really want to have a higher quality product that will sell well, you have to spend more.

Request for more product prototypes until you are 100% happy with the final product.

Step #5: Order your final product

Once you are happy with the quality of the product prototype, order the minimum quantity you can afford. The higher the quantity, the cheaper the production price you can get.

Step #6: Purchase a unique EAN and UPC barcodes

The final step in the production process is to purchase a unique EAN and UPC barcodes for your products. You can get it from **www.barcodestalk.co.uk** and other similar websites. Unique EAN and UPC barcodes are needed in order for you to sell on Amazon.

2. How to Ship Inventory to Amazon Fulfillment Centers

Step #7: Find a reliable freight forwarder

Dealing with customs, shipping charges, and all the different taxes is a total problem. Fortunately, there are many companies, referred to as freight forwarders, which could handle everything on your behalf. You simply connect your forwarder with your manufacturer and they can get all the details taken care of.

This is the general workflow how Freight forwarders send your products to Amazon fulfillment centers:

- The manufacturer (in China) sends the inventory FOB (freight on board).

- The freight forwarder obtains the products from China to their storage warehouse in your target country.

- The freight forwarder completes all your customs documents.

- You make payment for your customs taxes (usually through your freight forwarder).

- You generate the pre-paid shipping labels from Amazon Seller Central and mail them to your selected freight forwarder. Some freight forwarders can even print the barcode labels for you.

- The freight forwarder sticks the labels to your FBA inventory and sends them to the various Amazon FBA warehouses.

You can check the following freight forwarders and their services and see which one can best satisfy your requirements:

- **ForestShipping - Frequently Asked Questions for FBA shipment:** http://forestshipping.com/faq/
- **RiversourceLogistics - How It Works:** http://riversourcelogistics.com/process-steps/, **Support Center:** http://riversourcelogistics.com/faq-support-center/

- **AdstralFulfilment - Amazon Fulfillment:** http://www.adstralfulfilment.co.uk/ebay-fulfilment.html
- **Shapiro - Amazon FBA:** http://www.shapiro.com/amazon-fba/
- **FBAforward - Services:** http://fbaforward.com/services.php
- **AMZtransit - Services:** http://amztransit.com/#our-services

YouTube Video Tutorials
- **Amazon FBA Inspection and Importing from China Best Practices by River Source Logistics:** https://goo.gl/SDgV2h
- **Amazon FBA Inspection Services with River Source Logistics - How to Create an LTL Shipment to Amazon:** https://goo.gl/nAKV9f
- **Amazon FBA Inspection services with River Source Logistics - Receiving Container Load:** https://goo.gl/zeSPCK
- **How To Get Your Product From China To Amazon FBA:** https://goo.gl/KhzwUd
- **Getting Your Product From China To Amazon FBA:** https://goo.gl/BjCg3b
- **Tips For Sourcing Private Label Products In China:** https://goo.gl/3f8rd8
- **Shipping from China to Amazon FBA: Freight Forwarders:** https://goo.gl/dYQJMy

3. Private label Production Timeline

If you think about it, it's actually not very complicated to have a product created and sell it on Amazon. But it's a lot harder and requires much more time to earn any cash from it!

This is the timeline to get a product designed and made in China.

- Searching and choosing a factory usually takes at the very least 2 to 3 weeks.

- Presenting and describing to them your product design and receiving a prototype and product samples delivered, tested and modified is going to take around one to two months.

- As soon as you set your first order, just for them to produce it should take a minimum of an additional month.

- To deliver it to your country, get pass around customs and getting it to the Amazon FBA facilities may take no less than an additional two months (if delivery is done by ship from China to the US).

- The moment you started selling on Amazon, normally it takes some time to gain some results, accumulate reviews and start to get really good everyday income.

- Now at long last, you have got some amount of money in your bank account, but then you are likewise running out on your initial stock and so you are required to invest that initial income you have on your bank on the second product order.

Normally, it will take a year before you could take sizable money through this technique. To succeed using the "Private label technique", you will need both of these: a substantial sum of starting money along with the patience and perseverance to wait for several months without an income.

When starting selling at Amazon FBA, you don't need to go right away through this route. If you're new to selling on amazon, you can use "Sourcing from online wholesale stores" and "Sourcing from Local Product Sources" techniques.

d. The Needs of a Manufacturer / Supplier

Once you've found a reliable supplier and maintained a profitable and reciprocal agreement, you will have to find ways to upgrade and improve that relationship. Suppliers are difficult to come by these days; you can find one great connection after dozens of failed attempts. Therefore, cherish that attachment by supplementing the bond with various elements.

Supplier behavior is vital to your business. The qualities of the products they deliver reflect your brand. Suppliers need valuable assets and here are some tips for you:

- **Move your business relationship to a more personalized one.** Once you know your suppliers very well in how they work, you can stick with them and have a long term business relationship which can help provide larger discounts and better deals.

- **Proper payment and decorum when encountering problems.** It is also a must to estimate orders within enough timeframe that won't rush or pressure the delivery. It would ultimately affect the quality of the product.

- **Use technology to increase efficiency by organizing your products, as well as to monitor the dynamic demand of the market.** In addition, learn how to use the online system provided by Amazon and other FBA apps to supervise the input and output of products to prevent misunderstanding with order placements and other complications.

- **Provide your suppliers with up-to-date feedbacks on product innovations.** As soon as customer reviews are starting to coming in, you should send them the feedbacks and necessary product modifications to improve your product line.

YouTube Video Tutorial
- **How to negotiate the best price on your Private Label Product:** https://goo.gl/sutcd4
- **Importing from China - Sourcing Products from Chinese Suppliers:** https://goo.gl/6NYFkJ
- **How to Source Products from China to Resell - Expert Interview:** https://goo.gl/6aJbdU
- **Dealing with a Chinese supplier:** https://goo.gl/CPw5dE
- **Sending Payment for your first Private Label Product:** https://goo.gl/RuHbtw

e. How to Test Suppliers?

In this section, I would like to discuss briefly how to determine whether the supplier is reliable or not. The best-case scenario would be is to have a reliable supplier and maintaining an equally beneficial partnership. The worst-case scenario, however, would be to trust them with your business and money and then realize that they're a sham.

Here are the eight questions you can apply to test your suppliers:

1 - The Manufacturers Real Identity:

Who really are your manufacturers? Get a background check on their standing in comparison to other product competitors. Research about their reputation, and check different reviews about the quality of their services if available online.

2 - The Manufacturer's Business Longevity:

How long have they been in business? You can determine their market performance by the length of time they've been in business and how they've overcome global economic decline.

3 - The Manufacturer's Size Of Business:

How big are they in terms of revenues, factory size, etc.? You can check whether the supplier would be able to cater to your demand or not.

4 - The Manufacturer's ISO Certification:

Are they legally allowed to conduct business? This certificate guarantees a supplier's lawful production of goods as they go through the compliance of standard requirements in a business.

5 - The Manufacturer's Compliance With International Standards:

Do they comply with standards around the world? Conforming to international standards further assures the company's legitimacy and quality of their products produced.

6 - The Manufacturer's Experience With Their Product:

Are they up-to-date with the technology and knowledge? If they use the latest technology and methods in producing their products, then it shows that you can rely on the supplier's quality assurance for producing quality products, thus improving your business direction.

7 - The Manufacturer's International Recognitions:

What are their achievements in the global trade community? International recognitions will prove their quality manifestations in the larger market.

8 - The Manufacturer's Supply Chain:

Are the raw materials in good quality? You can also assess the quality of the materials they use in their products. The consistency of quality from raw materials to manufacturing will ensure excellence in the merchandise itself.

YouTube Video Tutorials
- **How to Communicate with Overseas Manufacturers:** https://goo.gl/VpBfpD
- **How to Choose The Right Manufacturer to Private Label your Product:** https://goo.gl/6cHPNb
- **How to Find the Best Products to Sell on Amazon & Find High Quality, Low Cost Suppliers:** https://goo.gl/u6TI64
- **Exactly How I'm Making $2,500 Per Month Selling On Amazon FBA:** https://goo.gl/5EM9B7
- **Dealing with a Chinese supplier:** https://goo.gl/fVTfQw

CHAPTER 5: HOW TO SELL YOUR PRODUCT?

There are many different ways to sell your product. We can try the old door-to-door salesman method, opening a store of our own or setting up an e-commerce website. Sadly, all these options require a lot of initial capital and are time-consuming. The best option would be, is to sell on Amazon. It's very easy to get started, the traffic is already there and you can start with just one product.

Amazon is one of the most visited websites in the world and is a great place to sell products. Marketing requires strategy and effort so you don't lose your product in the myriad of other products available on the website.

Since putting together your own e-commerce website is difficult, we will use Amazon as our own website. You will get the chance to sell online even with only just one product and you will always have the opportunity to add more items to your line up as you go on.

There a few aspects of Amazon to consider when selling a product. Firstly, when a buyer will search for a product such as "Headphones" Amazon will take the customer to a page where all headphones available on the website can be seen. Meaning that if you are selling a product, that another 20 business are selling as well then your chances of the buyer choosing your product are very low, especially if your product is expensive. There's a popular "buy box" for sellers with the best prices and selling history that is highlighted for customers. If you just started selling a product then most likely you will not be within the "buy box" lowering your chances of selling even more.

The best strategy to make a profit would be market a unique product or resell an item that is uniquely made by someone else. Based on experience it is always a bad idea to sell videos and music. Many of these products are usually obtained free online. Another thing to consider is the pricing you set on your products when using Amazon. There's a monthly fee from Amazon as well as shipping services. By setting a fair price for your product, you will ensure your profits won't be lost.

Even though we are using Amazon to sell our products, we can always advertise our products on other websites. It'll boost sales if we write descriptive content about our products because it will build trust and bring ease to potential buyers when they are considering your product.

We can post our product details on Facebook or go further and manage a Blog about the product. This way, buyers won't use Amazon to search for your product but directly buy.

Another GREAT feature from selling with Amazon is the FBA (Fulfillment by Amazon) where they will take care of shipping and storage of your product. It is manageable dealing with 10 orders a day but once your business grows then you will have to handle hundreds of orders, shipping, and possible returns. With FBA you can ship your products to an Amazon warehouse for storage, they ship your products to every individual customer, Amazon will cover all shipping and handling, and any returns or customer service is taken care of by Amazon as well. For the seller this means you can work while not doing much, you don't have to deal with the stress of returns, and no need to hire employees and you will be able to sell more of your product. You don't have to use FBA but I highly recommend it.

We have two general types of markets: one with **high competition** and one with **low competition.** If you choose a product in a market that has high competition then making a profit will be difficult since buyers have many options to choose from. Picking a product from a not very competitive market will give you a better chance of making sales. However, there are usually a higher number of buyers inside a competitive market but the sales are distributed among the competitors. Even though a less competitive market has a lower amount of buyers, solely by chance they will choose your product since there are fewer options.

a. Listing Your Product On Amazon

Listing on products on Amazon is very easy and straightforward. The trick is to know how the Amazon algorithm works. Firstly let's go over how to actually get your products listed without going into listing strategy. Listing from the "Product Page" is the simplest way for first-time sellers to start. Find the equivalent product on the Amazon site and then choose "Sell Yours." There are four ways to search for your product, which is through the Universal Pin Code (UPC), International Standard Book Number (ISBN), European Article Number (EAN) or just searching by name. Just make the sure product you find is identical to the one you are planning on selling.

If your product is made from scratch and not imported then Listing via "Seller Central" works well too. If your product is already listed on Amazon then in Seller Central go to the Inventory Tab and choose "Add a Product." You will then enter the UPC or ISBN in the Product ID field and your product on Amazon will appear. Check to see if your product matches the search results. To finalize everything just enter the seller Stock Keeping Unit, condition, notes, prices and quantity and wrap everything up by clicking on "Save and Finish." If your product is NOT listed on Amazon then simply click on "Create a New Product" and provide all the info necessary for your product to be listed.

YouTube Video Tutorials
- **Organizing and Listing Inventory:**
  https://goo.gl/yHZCw4
- **How To List FBA Items Through Amazon Seller Central:** https://goo.gl/5uvFqZ
- **Steps by Step Process for Getting Inventory Ready for Amazon FBA Shipment:** https://goo.gl/TdRkCD

b. Preparing your Product Information

When you need to create a listing for an item that doesn't exist in the Amazon catalog, it is very important that you write a great description. You can ensure this happens by preparing the information of your product beforehand.

The description is not the first thing a potential buyer will see of your product while browsing on Amazon, but if they are interested they will carefully read it to see if the item is exactly what they are looking for. People can be really careful while shopping online, and oftentimes a good description is the reason that pushes them to buy a product.

YouTube Video Tutorials
- **How to build out your Product Page on Amazon:**
  https://goo.gl/YrY1xB
- **Best Practices for Creating Product Detail Page:**
  https://goo.gl/72cpek

These are some tips you can follow to make sure your description stands out from the crowd.

1 - Title

Don't use the title as a description page. The title should only be the product name, don't use fancy words and make sure it's short. Amazon is now cracking down products that abuse the product title by stuffing too much keyword.

When creating a title, be sure to add your brand name. By doing so, your product will become more search-friendly and you can capture even more customers that are looking for a particular brand name. If the manufacturer number is available, you should add that to the title as well.

2 - Features / Bullet Points

Features, which will be shown as bullet points underneath the pricing and product options, are a complete requirement.

Much like with photos, Features are extremely important to Amazon that they no longer permit products without bullet points to be featured in the buy box. Not having Features is a significant roadblock to achieving good rankings on Amazon.

Features should be extremely detailed and should contain a huge amount of keywords.

On the other hand, they must be effortlessly readable, so it won't confuse customers and risk hurting conversions.

A good example of the proper use of the Feature section is **this Asus computer monitor**, which is top-rated in the "computer screen" keyword.

Asus computer monitor product page:
http://goo.gl/Sm4mZg

3 - Description

Your product description is really the place where you elaborate on your product Features. It's also the section of the page that you have the most control over. If there's place to seriously place significant effort into to engage customers, it's definitely in the product description section.

Keep in mind, there is no need to write keywords multiple times on your product page. Just make sure your description is at least 1000 words long. Talk about your product benefits, customer problems, and solutions your product can offer.

A good example of the proper use of the Feature section is **this DeLhongi Espresso Maker**, which is rank#1 in the "Semi-Automatic Espresso Machines" category.

DeLhongi Espresso Maker product page:
http://goo.gl/UMQPH2

4 - Category

When you list your product, be sure to add your product inventory in the most appropriate and most specific category available. Decide wisely about where your item belongs and make sure you pick the right category and sub-category.

YouTube Video Tutorials

- **Listing and Packaging Your First Shipment:** https://goo.gl/WDMsQX
- **Starting An Amazon FBA Business - The Complete Series:** https://goo.gl/GQefTQ

c. Steps In Writing Product Descriptions

A well-trained salesman in the real world has the task and capability to persuade the customer to buy their products over their competitor's products. The same goes for Amazon FBA. As an online seller, it is your job to sell your products.

So, how do we go about writing a well-written product description?

Here are the steps you'll need in achieving this:

STEP #1: Know You Buyer's Persona

What is buyer persona? This is an imaginary customer. This person will be the person whom you have developed and now want to sell your products to. He or she will be representing the target audience you want to achieve.

As a seller, this is essential knowledge to obtain. You will need to know what your target audience so well that you will understand what makes them want to click on your product and what makes him or her hesitate to purchase.

In order for you to start describing your buyer persona, make an understanding of what he or she is reading and which sites she visits. This is important as it will aid you in understanding the tone of voice you would want to be projecting in your description.

Take into consideration:

1. How they make decisions?

2. What keeps them awake at night?

3. What they may consider achieving?

Gaining knowledge into this will allow you to create a description that speaks to him or her and taps into their feelings.

Defining the persona provides you the information you will need to transform product-centric descriptions into that of a customer-centric description. Visualizing how your customer is will empower you as a seller to creating descriptions that are vivid and persuasive.

STEP #2: Creating A List Of Features And Benefits

As a seller of your products, you should love to talk about them.

Maybe it's a product that you have been searching that has such a high potential to become bestselling items. You should take joy in enumerating to people the specified details, features, and specifications.

Your clients may want to learn what your product is or does. They are keen on understanding what they benefit and how their lives benefit from purchasing the product.

When starting on your writing, it helps to start on the list of all the features and your product specifications. With that information, you can turn them into benefits.

A **feature** generally talks about the facts of your products, while a **benefit** is an explanation of how the feature can be an advantage to the customer.

A benefit can be phrased as a positive, which may improve or increase what your customer is looking for or a problem that can be avoided, for example, less stress.

STEP #3: Define Your Tone of Voice

You don't want to come across to your customer as a person who is a boring big corporation that just wants to sell its products for money. What you're aiming for is to engage your readers with some personality and a dash of humor.

Creating a persuasive tone of voice may differentiate you from that of your competitors. In the end, it will give your readers a strong impression of your organization's personality and its culture.

Make sure that your personality shines through the written content and don't hesitate to add some side comments for humor. Rather than remark that the customer service that you provide is excellent, allow your tone of voice to demonstrate that you're friendly, approachable and interesting towards understanding your clients business.

Once you understand your buyer persona, creating the first draft becomes a breeze.

With the list of features and benefits as well as your persona in mind, you should be able to create a comprehensive and persuasive product description.

YouTube Video Tutorials
- **Amazon Product Description Writing Tutorial:** https://goo.gl/ZUQrWs
- **95% of Amazon Sellers are Making This 1 Simple Mistake:** https://goo.gl/dtyxcV

d. Using Pictures

They say an image says more than a thousand words, and when it comes to online selling they are absolutely right. When using images, make sure you take a nice and well-lit picture of your product. Read and follow **Amazon guidelines for pictures** so you don't get any of them deleted.

Amazon guidelines for pictures: http://goo.gl/ZfNGuZ

Quality pictures are very important in getting people into buying your products. We are going to want one large and high-quality image that will provide the buyer with all the information he visually needs instead of multiple normal sized images. This is because Amazon has a zoom feature that will allow the user to view your image up close so the better the image quality the clearer the buyer can see your image when zoomed in.

You can upload up to eight pictures. Use them wisely to show every angle of your product. It is also recommended to show the product in action if possible.

Things to Avoid with Amazon Pictures:

Amazon is very strict with product photos. Follow the following rules to avoid being banned in Amazon.

1 - Advertising text
Never place an advertising text on your pictures which Amazon will consider as a violation. Eliminate any kind of messaging that has words like "Sale", "Free Shipping", or an equivalent marketing appearance.

2 - Colored Primary Photo Background
Primary pictures should have a pure white background. Pure white background blends in with the amazon website search and product detail pages.

3 - Colors, Drawings, Watermarks
These are the other things you are not allowed to have on your product photos

- Displaying one picture showing multiple product color selections even though they are sold separately

- Making use of line drawings or cartoons

- Putting in animated pictures

- Adding watermarks on photos

Be sure to review and double-check out all your product photos with Amazon's picture specifications before you begin selling on Amazon. To find out more on Amazon picture policies, check out **Amazon's product image specifications.**

Amazon's product image specifications:
http://goo.gl/xiQTK9

YouTube Video Tutorials
- **Do you need to take photos of the products you are selling on amazon FBA?:** https://goo.gl/8bFTkj
- **How To Take High Quality Pictures For Amazon That Will Double Your Sales!:** https://goo.gl/tB3ytD
- **Creating an Amazon FBA photo studio for CHEAP-taking great photos!:** https://goo.gl/sqS3w3

e. Pricing And Repricing Strategies

As mentioned previously, pricing is vital in ensuring a successful business career through Amazon. The proper use of different pricing styles will determine whether you've maximized your profit or not. These are the three main pricing strategies that you should take into consideration before pricing your items.

The following will provide the pros and cons as well as the general application of each pricing tool.

3 Pricing & Repricing Strategies

1 - Manual

- **APPLICATION:** This technique is most preferable for those of you selling in small quantities. It is more suitable for those authentic items with little to no competition in the Amazon market because there are no other supplies that you have to adjust your prices accordingly. Another type of suppliers that should use manual are those who are reselling products that have a fixed price from manufacturers. You can manually alter a price through a third party or at the Amazon Seller Central.

- **PROS:** You're able to manipulate the prices to your precise control and will be made available to you since alteration is relatively simple to accomplish. At small amounts, this would be straightforward and supervised.

- **CONS:** If you have a large inventory that needs Repricing, manual Repricing isn't for you. It takes up a lot of time and effort and can be subject to a human error affecting the chain of distribution.

2 - Rule-Based

- **APPLICATION:** In rule-based Repricing, the main focus is to comply with protocol when applying the prices to your products. After assessing your competition prices, there are various sets of rules to choose from and to implement. One example could be to surpass the competition by one dollar. This type of Repricing is perfect for people who aren't entitled to the Buy Box feature and who sell items with low profit in return. A few examples of these items would be goods related to media and books.

- **PROS:** This strategy is very easy to implement because your pricing strategy will just react to any price changes within the competition and will make sure you have a minimum mark-up for each product you sell.

- **CONS:** It's time-consuming at first and needs a correct understanding of product pricing to get it right when you're making up the rules to fit with your needs.

3 - Apps-Based

- **APPLICATION:** Apps-Based repricing is a more sophisticated way of finding a more favorable price by using a smartphone app. What it does is that it calculates the maximum profit you can attain with each product based on the Buy Box share.

- **PROS:** It's automatic and, once installed, is effortless to use. This would be an ideal way of repricing the products, as you would expect to acquire higher profit and having the lowest labor to set up.

- **CONS:** To install Repricing apps is easy, but requires a monthly subscription. For those with smaller businesses that can't afford it, they should try other options.

f. How to Price Products Correctly

The mistake that online business personnel or even people who sell products in general may carry out without even knowing is the factor of pricing their product. Some don't even know their products worth and assume that what they pay for the products is what the customers will pay for as well.

When wanting to achieve a fair price that customers would generally not mind paying for, this is the wrong direction to go.

Ask yourself these questions:
- Do you really understand how much your product is worth?

- How low are you, as a seller, willing to price an item in order to compete with other e-commerce salesmen?

Here are given tips that you should use as an e-commerce seller in order to achieve the fair price for your products:

1 - The Simple Formula
Most retailers, both virtually and real life, use the pricing strategy known as *Keystone Pricing*, this essentially means that you will double the cost of the product obtaining a 50% markup.

Although, this may not be the case, you may want to mark-up your products either lower or higher in relation to your specific situation.

Here is a simple to follow formula to acquire the right retail price to sell your product:

Retail Price = [(Cost of Item) / (100 – markup percentage)] x 100

For example, let's say you receive a product you want to price that costs you $15 at a 45% markup rather than using the usual 50%. Here's how you would calculate it:

Retail Price = [(15.00) / 100 – 45)] x 100

Retail Price = (15.00 / 55) x 100 = $27.00

2 - Understanding Margins

In the reality of online retail pricing, the lowest price doesn't generally win. In fact, some people may usually end up pricing their products way too low. Even with the amount of customers that you are attracting, you may not be gaining any profits.

When you lower your product prices to the point where you won't be gaining or even losing money from the costs, then consider searching for a better source or you can decide to adjust your product offerings to include your more profitable items.

When your store goes into a pricing battle, this may hurt your business in the long-term. With consistently low prices, your customers may always expect that your prices will continue to go lower even when they are either aware or unaware of your business unsustainability.

This results in losing customers over time.

3 - Be Aware of your USP (Unique Selling Proposition)

This is where you ask yourself, what makes you different from all the other competitors?

Every person running a business must tackle this question and determine their businesses value proposition and target market.

Usually, for online retailers, a unique factor of maximizing their ability with customer services uses free shipping of products that can be delivered within days, which is what Amazon Prime is for or products sold that you can't find anywhere.

In the online market world, pricing competition is an all-time high. As a seller, you should think of products that may be out of the box that would still be a demand in the market when you craft your marketing strategy for your online store.

4 - Lose-Leader Strategy (Selling Products Below Market Value)

When going into highly discounted pricing, it would become a great advantage if only in the use of an appropriate merchandise strategy.

What will be explained here is the *Lose-Leader* Strategy. This strategy would assume that your item sold below the market value will encourage your customers to buy more products *overall*. In using this strategy, online store owners will gain the opportunity to upsell, cross-sell and even increase the total sum of shopping cart value that a customer will purchase online. (Otherwise, known as average revenue per user)

5 - Put Forward Incentives

Once you are able to understand your margins as well as pricing your products accordingly, you are capable of offering incentives in order to create motivation for your customers to purchase your products.

TIP: As an FBA seller, you can set up your own promotions. Just go to **Seller Central**, click **Advertising** > **Manage Promotions**.

By going to the Seller Central, you can set eligible products to the following promotions:

1. Money Off: for each item they purchased, they will get a specific cash discount.

2. Buy One, Get One: for each item purchased, they will get another identical item for free.

3. External Benefits: when they purchase an item, they will get an after-purchase benefit, such as a cash discount on the next purchase of the same item.

Semantics may become of importance in this area as the language and words you use may attract more customers.

- When you have a product that is surplus, then you can consider taking the strategy of the *'twofer'*, which basically means two for one.

- Some customers may perceive large percentages as big savings. For example, *"Buy one; get the second one at 50%"*. Customers perceive the 50% off, but in reality, they're just getting 25% discount.

Being witty about your incentives gives you the ability to attract attention to your products and build reputations on offering good deals without having to lost profits.

You may not make a lot of money at the beginnings of your Amazon business. It can be a long journey to success, but there are ways to accelerate this by implementing strategies that will lead you to the top of Amazon sellers.

g. Amazon FBA Seller Pricing And Repricing Tools

Determining how much to sell a product becomes easy with the use of pricing and repricing tools. These are used by sellers to list, scout and reprice products.

To begin with, let's consider Amazon's native app.

Amazon Seller App

Amazon has now created its own seller app to help Amazon sellers. The Amazon Seller mobile app can make your life easier as an Amazon sellers to instantly update your FBA inventory, find and list new products online and answer customer inquiries.

The following are the Amazon Seller app features that make this app useful:

- **Update Inventory** - Easily manage your Amazon FBA inventory: You can find, sort and filter product items, update your selling prices and change item quantities quickly from your mobile phone.

- **Source New Items To Sell** - By entering product names or scanning barcodes, you can now compare existing selling prices, product sales rank and the customer reviews of the specific products on Amazon.

- **Calculate The Potential Earning Of Products Before Selling** - Add product price information to find out the expected potential earning of products.

- **List New Products To Sell** - Make new product listings on Amazon instantly and conveniently.

- **Respond To Customers Inquiries** - Give impressive customer support by replying quickly to customers inquiries.

- **View your current earnings** - See how much earnings you currently have and when you'll get paid by Amazon.

- **Get Assistance from Amazon** - Use the app to get in touch with seller assistance using email or chat.

Download the Amazon Seller App: If you want to try the Amazon Seller app, you can download it for free. You can **get it from Google Play** for Android, **Apple for iOS** and also **from the Amazon App Store** if you are using an Amazon device.

Google App Store: https://goo.gl/SasBGu
Apple App Store: https://goo.gl/cWHA9c
Amazon App Store: http://goo.gl/HrrDGA

Choosing which seller app to work with is solely based on personal taste and preference. In some cases, there are some important features that you can get from non-Amazon apps. However, it will require you to spend more. If you are just okay with that, you can find out below which app can work best for you and your budget.

1. Listing Tools

Listing of products through the Amazon Seller Central can be time-consuming especially if you'll be listing more than 50 items a month. Listing tools are used to automate and speed up the process of putting up your inventory on Amazon.

- **ASellertool** - This allows you to batch large quantity of items all at once and it supports FBA shipment management and label printing. You can register the Amazon Batch Listing software after registering your **Amazon MWS** (Marketplace Web Service) account to Asellertool service.

  ASellertool page:
  http://www.asellertool.com/listing.html

- **Listtee** - This tool offers a simple listing software that links to all US and UK Amazon FBA warehouses. With this tool, you can replenish items and print single labels. It also has a feature on SKU detection to avoid listing of the same item twice, thus reduce listing errors.

Listtee website: http://www.listtee.com/

- **Neatoscan** - This tool is used to sell on multiple platforms. If later on, you decide to sell aside from your Amazon Seller account, then you may try the **Inventory Manager** tool. This tool integrates your online business so you can save time and costs while increasing productivity. The features include prescanning and receiving, inventory management, shipping, reports and FBA integration.

  Neatoscan page:
  http://www.neatoscan.com/InventoryManager.aspx

2. Scouting Tools

Getting a good product should be your main goal whenever you want to list an item on Amazon. To help you make wise decisions about potential inventory, you can use scouting tools. Most of the listing tools are integrated with its scouting tool so that after scouting, the listing could be easy and quick to accomplish.

- **Asellertool FBAscan** - This App is for Android or iPhone gadgets, which can help you in checking the Amazon pricing information by scanning or entering the item's barcode. One good advantage of this App is that it has two scouting modes, the Local Database, and Live Search. The former requires no internet connection or can be used in areas with poor signal wherein the price information is stored in your phone, while the latter is used with internet connection and get real-time Amazon price information including those not found in local databases.

Asellertool FBAscan page:
http://www.asellertool.com/products/fba-scan.html

- **Listtee Scout Rabbit** - This App can be availed from Listtee Pro and Enterprise Lite plans. It is another App to bring you the basic FBA pricing data as well as sales rank across all Amazon categories. When scouting for items, product barcodes can be read by Bluetooth scanner, a phone camera and by typing the name of the product.

  Listtee Scout Rabbit page:
  http://www.listtee.com/pricing/

- **Neatoscan** - Neatoscan has another tool, the **Neatopricer.** This tool utilizes a barcode scanner and PDA or iPhone/Android device without a need for internet connection. This helps you to have a quick and easy way to determine the value of the merchandise. It requires you to download first the PDA before you scan all categories.

Neatoscan page:
http://www.neatoscan.com/HowItWorks.aspx

- **SellerEngine Profit-bandit App** - This App is considered as the #1 mobile Amazon seller software, which is downloaded either for iPhone or Android phones. Profit Bandit is a tool that helps seller maximize profit, keep an eye on the competition, and save time while making money. Using this App will help you find how much profit you can make from the item you want to sell. It scans the barcode and computes the cost including the FBA fees and you'll get the possible profit.

SellerEngine Profit-bandit App page:
http://sellerengine.com/profit-bandit/

- **Scanpower Scout** - This App provides a real-time data from Amazon and access to the entire catalog. A very useful App because of the information it provides that include data of other FBA sellers such as the number they are selling and the net price after taking out Amazon fees.

Scanpower Scout page:
http://www.scanpower.com/features/scanpower
-scouting/

- **Scoutpal** - There are two tools that can be used from Scoutpal: the Instant Lookups with a PDA and Live Lookups with a phone. The tools are simple and easy to use whenever you scout for items. You only need to enter the ISBNs or UPCs of an item and the tool will get the information you need. If you have a scanner attached to your device, you can scan it instead of entering the data. Then, you'll see information on the lowest prices in used/new/collectible lists, Amazon price, and sales rank. More so, the Live results will show the market prices and quantities, editions and availability. To easily comprehend the report, you can customize the content and format the details according to your preference.

Scoutpal page: http://www.scoutpal.com/sp/

3. Repricing Tools

With a dynamic marketplace such as the Amazon, updating and keeping your inventory with the right price is necessary. Repricing tools help you automate the process by selecting your criteria and reprice a large number of items within a short amount of time. Most of the repricing tools are offered with a listing tool such as the NeatoScan Inventory Manager; it is advisable that you evaluate every part of the features and go for the best App for you.

- **RepriceIt** - This tool is a cloud-based system, thus, no software needs to be downloaded. You can access your account anywhere with internet connection. This tool allows you to schedule repricing more frequently during peak buying times on Amazon while experimenting with different repricing strategies. Most importantly, this tool has full FBA support and you'll get detailed repricing reports onto your email.

RepriceIt page:
http://www.repriceit.com/welcome.do

- **ScanPower** -This App is used by sellers when listing items to sell. It has different features like Evaluate and Reprice for great use of sellers. These features help you calculate the prices based on FBA net price, which includes the price and shipping.

ScanPower website:
http://www.scanpower.com/

- **Sellery** - This tool from SellerEngine is used to help sellers compete and maximize profits. It features the Sellery's on-demand, per item pricing preview where you can create new pricing rules, pick any item in your inventory and preview your pricing strategies. With this App, you can prevent price mistakes because floor price calculation is automated and item-specific. It includes Amazon fees, FBA and shipping costs aside from the margin you want so you can come up with an accurate minimum price.

Sellery page: http://sellerengine.com/sellery/

Amazon FBA Tools are definitely a must-have on your phone when you start selling on Amazon. An extra fee for the Apps will ensure that you are pricing your items properly and competitively on Amazon. No need to guess any price for your item. If you want to get the highest possible margin for your inventory, make sure that your pricing is calculated based on accurate data and information.

h. Materials Needed For Your Shipment

Starting out selling on Amazon will require a few materials that are needed in order to send your products to an Amazon warehouse. Some tools are very necessary while others will just make your life as a seller easier. Investing in tools that will increase productivity is a great idea and should be considered.

1 - Boxes

Let's begin with materials that are necessary. We're going to need shipping boxes. For your first shipment I recommend you collect free boxes from anywhere you can get them such as local stores, Craigslist and friends are all good options. Once you begin sending more and more shipments are required then buying boxes would be a better idea. All home improvement stores sell boxes that are perfect for FBA. Try and stick with small or medium boxes and only use large boxes if your shipment will be bulky.

2 - Packing Tape

Packing Tape and a Tape Gun are going to very important tools to pack your boxes together. You can buy these anywhere and at a cheap price. If you start shipping out more boxes then consider buying tape in bulk instead of single rolls. The minimum tape size that you should use is 2.2 mil. However, those tapes that are bigger and larger will stick better on the box.

3 - Measuring Tape

You need to measure the boxes you are about to send out to Amazon. Every box needs to be measured before you print a shipping label. You can get an inexpensive measuring tape at your local thrift store. Many retail stores have some affordable ones.

4 - Printer

The Dymo Label Printer is perfect for FBA labels and you will save money since you won't be buying ink anymore. However, for starters, you can use a toner laser printer since their prints don't smudge.

For the complete printing and labeling information, please see Amazon's **printing guidelines**.

Printing guideline page: http://goo.gl/CT311M

5 - Labels

For printing your product label barcodes, you will need a standard 30-up address label. I highly recommend the Avery 18160 and 5160 address labels. However, you could also find other generic address labels that will work as good as the branded one.

If you don't want to spend more money, printing your barcodes on a white blank sheet of paper and using a tape to stick them on the boxes, can work as well. However, the time and effort for you to do it yourself are not so worth it. Address labels are just cheap, just buy them and save yourself from trouble.

Just make sure your labels are printed and placed properly on your boxes or products.

To learn more about proper labeling, please view this YouTube tutorial by Amazon: **How to Label Products for Fulfillment by Amazon:** https://goo.gl/34YTKm.

6 - Scales
Shipping scales are going to be needed to accurately calculate the weight for your boxes. At first using a bathroom or a kitchen scale will work fine but I highly recommend a shipping scale to properly weigh your products.

7 - Poly Bags
Consider as well having the poly bags since you will need to put many of your products enclosed with poly bags.

With these items, you will have what is needed for shipping. It may be a little costly at first but these are only initial investments that will surely pay off in the long run. Always remember to follow all of Amazon's rules and regulations.

YouTube Video Tutorials
- **How I Package Items For Amazon FBA - Save Money & Clear Up Misconceptions:** https://goo.gl/N6hX8J
- **4 best packing materials for shipping Amazon items:** https://goo.gl/rYUHbu
- **How to make custom shipping boxes for Amazon FBA:** https://goo.gl/wr6y7K

- **Tips for Packing Materials and Supplies for shipping on Amazon:** https://goo.gl/pPgtHr
- **Amazon FBA Rules, Guidelines, and Supplies:** https://goo.gl/9eEP2V
- **Packaging Your First Shipment:** https://goo.gl/WDMsQX
- **Finalizing Your First Shipment:** https://goo.gl/WPgtMr

i. How to Create Amazon FBA Labels

Each of the units that you will be sending to Amazon for the fulfillment requires a uniquely scannable barcode that will enable and ensure easy storage once it reaches the fulfillment center.

If you have a barcode for a product that is not unique (For example: If you have a barcode for a product that comes in various different colors and sizes) then you should use a different UPC, EAN or FNSKU label that can be printed, through your Seller Central account.

Here are label requirements for Amazon FBA, this guide will provide as a great way to ensure that prompt and precise labeling for all of your product units:

1 - Basic Labeling Requirements

If you do not want the choice of applying these labels by yourself, then you can sign up for **Stickerless Commingled Inventory** or another choice of the **FBA Label Service** to do the service for you.

Stickerless Commingled Inventory page:
http://goo.gl/pA3azs
FBA Label Service page: http://goo.gl/nFn2qM

If you want to change your account from the stickerless, commingled inventory to becoming a labeled inventory, then you will need to follow these steps:

1. Go to your settings > *Click Fulfillment by Amazon* > *Choose Inventory Settings* (Stickerless Commingled Inventory)

2. Select the 'Edit' button that can be found in the *Choose Inventory Settings*

3. Click the 'Disable' button and choose 'Save' in order to have this new setting placed.

Once you have changed this setting, you will need to go through the task of re-listing your products before you are able to send them to Amazon as labeled inventory.

The following are the requirements how to properly label your FBA product inventory:

TIP #1: Conceal Any Original Barcodes

- Cover any of the original manufacturer's barcode (UPC, EAN, ISBN)

- Make sure that no other barcodes can be scanned

- If there are failure to cover any barcodes placed then errors may occur and results in inventory loss

TIP 2#: Label Each Of The Units Prior To Sending It To Amazon

- Be aware that the label title matches to the corresponding unit. This will ensure that any merchandise can be received, stocked and sold

- Rule of thumb: Use only white labels that are a removable adhesive

Tip: All your labels should be able to be removed by the customers

TIP 3#: Do Not Do The Following

- **Do not use** faded labels on your desired units

- **Do not wrap** any of your labels around curves and/or corners on the unit as this would deem the label as unscannable

- **Do not leave** any other barcodes uncovered unless the unit has been established as stickerless and commingled inventory.

- **Do not use QR barcodes** on the labels that you are providing, since these barcodes cannot be read by all scanners

2 - Print Requirements:

- Put to use a thermal transfer or laser printer

- Clean your printer

3 - Print PDF Labels

Amazon has already provided a downloadable PDF guide to teach you **How to Label Products**. Follow this guide when printing labels.

How to Label Products guide:
https://goo.gl/rKu2AF

4 - Use Scanning And Shipping Program

Amazon encourages you to use their **Scan and Ship program**. This program is capable of eliminating the task of looking through an entire sheet of labels in search of the right one or clicking through different pages on your Seller Account to find the products that you desire to ship.

Scan and Ship program page:
http://goo.gl/CnKWE7

j. How To Ship Inventory to Amazon Fulfillment Centers

In this section, I will discuss more how to ship products to Amazon, since they are the ones who will handle individual shipping to buyers. All we have to do is send our products to the Amazon warehouse.

Before we ship anything to Amazon we need to make sure our products are packaged and labeled. We cannot just send them products with no encasing so make sure your product packing is secure.

Once the items are ready then we are going to have to pack them into boxes to be shipped to Amazon. Make sure to print shipping labels for your boxes that can be found in the Inventory section that will include a list of products within the box and the quantity.

It is very advisable to use as few boxes as possible to avoid any possible loss. Furthermore, make sure to protect your products when packing with foam, air pillows or sheets of paper. Finally, check the boxes to see if they are sealed and your products will not move during shipping. When it comes to choosing a carrier you are free to choose any carrier with any shipping speed you wish. Just make sure to provide the tracking numbers when using your own carrier.

As mentioned before, make sure to print shipping labels for all your boxes. Go to the Shipping Queue to print them out and attach the labels to the outside of the box. The labels will show the destination address and return address. In some cases, the tracking number can also be shown, if you are using an **Amazon carrier**. This will make sure that all your products are packaged for protection against any damage during shipping or storage and that all units follow Amazon's labeling and requirements.

Amazon carrier page: http://goo.gl/ykaXa6

When a product is shipped out to a customer your name does not appear on any item labels nor shipping labels but on the packing slip that will be found inside the box. This is the only reference the buyer has that the product came from you.

Amazon also accepts shipments from other countries to their warehouses. However, the seller will have to arrange the imports of his product, go through customs and lastly get the products delivered to an Amazon warehouse. Amazon will not serve as an importer for your imported products, they will not take responsibility for any taxes or fees related to your import nor will they provide a tax number for you. The seller is responsible for dealing with all government agencies that relate to his import and has to provide prepaid delivery to the Amazon warehouse. Also, Amazon does not provide any quality check to your products unless they are obviously and visibly damaged. If the item is labeled as "used" then it is understandable that it may have minor damages and will not be checked.

Dealing with customs, shipping charges, and all the different taxes is a total problem. Fortunately, there are many companies, referred to as freight forwarders, which could handle everything on your behalf. You simply connect your forwarder with your manufacturer and they can get all the details taken care of.

You can check the following freight forwarders and their services and see which one can best satisfy your requirements:

- **ForestShipping - Frequently Asked Questions for FBA shipment:** http://forestshipping.com/faq/
- **RiversourceLogistics - How It Works:** http://riversourcelogistics.com/process-steps/, **Support Center:** http://riversourcelogistics.com/faq-support-center/

- **AdstralFulfilment - Amazon Fulfillment:** http://www.adstralfulfilment.co.uk/ebay-fulfilment.html
- **Shapiro - Amazon FBA:** http://www.shapiro.com/amazon-fba/
- **FBAforward - Services:** http://fbaforward.com/services.php
- **AMZtransit - Services:** http://amztransit.com/#our-services

Once again, Amazon does its best to make selling as easy as possible. All you have to do is get your products to the warehouse in good condition while following the requirements set by Amazon and we will be good to go.

YouTube Video Tutorials
- **How Can A Freight Forwarder Help You With Importing Into Your Country?:** https://goo.gl/HCz6aT
- **How To Ship Products From China & Avoid Unexpected Costs:** https://goo.gl/XC5Ame
- **How to ship your order from the Manufacturer:** https://goo.gl/HcDd2S
- **A Basic Guide to Exporting: Selecting a Freight Forwarder:** https://goo.gl/CDBBX9
- **Shipping from China to Amazon FBA: Freight Forwarders:** https://goo.gl/aPJ83G
- **Freight forwarding for Amazon FBA sellers:** https://goo.gl/FZGcTZ

- **Amazon FBA Inspection and Importing from China Best Practices:** https://goo.gl/kmHsrH
- **How to ship your first product to Amazon FBA:** https://goo.gl/B3AbGa
- **How to Ship to One Amazon FBA Fulfillment Center:** https://goo.gl/YRdE6U

k. How Amazon Handle Returns And Warranty?

Returns are common in this business. Maybe the buyer expected your product to be different, possibly damaged due to everyday reasons or they decided they just don't want your product anymore. Don't let it affect the way you feel about your product nor the way you conduct business. As long as you are keeping returns at a minimum then you're doing just fine.

With that said, we must know how to handle returns and the procedures that come with them. Amazon has always made it easy for its customers when it comes to return, they will process the whole return. Once the product reaches Amazon they will determine if the product is eligible for return or not. They will however usually accept units if they are returned within a certain time frame.

When the customer is issued the returned then Amazon will charge your seller account for the product including any taxes in order to reimburse the returnee.

Now if the product is damaged and is found unsellable then Amazon will reimburse you, this also applies if the item was lost or never arrived at the buyer.

The **Customer Return Timeline** for most products is 30 days and 90 days for Baby products. For products that are returned within the timeline, they will firstly have the product checked for any damage that would make the product unsellable. Products that are still in sellable condition will be placed back into your inventory in the warehouse. While any products that appear to be damaged will not be placed back into your inventory and you will be fully reimbursed for the item. There are certain cases where Amazon will not take responsibility and you will not be reimbursed for the item.

Customer Returns page: http://goo.gl/wZ2Sbz

Amazon will always consider all cases that are returned outside the return timeline and from time to time accept returns. If Amazon decides to accept the return then the same procedure would be followed as if the item was returned within the timeline, you will be fully reimbursed as well.

Let's go over what makes an item sellable or unsellable. An item that is still sellable will be added back to your inventory while any items that are considered unsellable will be placed in your "Unfulfillable Inventory" if Amazon in certain cases does not reimburse you. An item is unsellable if it is not in the same condition that it was originally shipped as or if the product is opened, damaged, defective or special cases when Amazon finds your product unsuitable.

Amazon once again shows how they take care of everyone working with them. Returning is made easy for the buyer and the seller. Just remember that returns are part of being a seller so get through them smoothly and continue selling.

YouTube Video Tutorials
- **The Secret Methods to Launch a Product to the Top of the Rankings on Amazon:** https://goo.gl/PSDfbM
- **5 Mistakes I Made on Amazon when I First Started Selling (that cost me $10k in lost sales!):** https://goo.gl/Z5ehLE

CHAPTER 6: AMAZON FBA FEES

Along with your normal marketplace seller charges, the FBA service will add multiple fees that you must pay to enjoy the service. However, it is important that you don't see these fees as an incremental cost of selling on Amazon. The money you pay for the FBA service is an investment.

As your internet business grows, it will start demanding more effort from your part. Your operational costs will go up as you start needing more storage space. You will spend more time packaging and managing your shipments. You may need to do international shipments and this takes time from your hands.

With more people buying your products you will need to offer customer service and you may find yourself overwhelmed by the amount of requests you will need to answer, all of them in a timely manner.

By using the Fulfillment By Amazon service, you're taking a huge weight out of your shoulders.

- You won't have to worry about storage space, as Amazon will expand it every time it's needed.

- You will have the excellent customer service of Amazon on your side, and you can be calmed knowing your buyers are in good hands.

- Amazon will make sure your products get to the buyer no matter where they are, and you will never have to worry about spending a lot of time figuring out how to ship your product out of the country.

a. The Size Chart

All FBA fees are calculated using the size of your product as a reference. Amazon has a size tier system that you need to understand before taking a look at the fees on the service.

Size Tier	Longest Side	Median Side	Shortest Side	Length + Girth	Weight
Small Standard Size	15"	12"	0.75"	n/a	Media: 14 oz Non-media: 12 oz
Large Standard Size	18"	14"	8"	n/a	20 lb.
Small Oversize	60"	30"	n/a	130"	70 lb.
Medium Oversize	108"	n/a	n/a	130"	150 lb.
Large Oversize	108"	n/a	n/a	165"	150 lb.
Special Oversize	Over 108"	n/a	n/a	Over 165"	Over 150 lb.

b. The Core Fees

These are the fees that you will pay for every single product that gets processed by the FBA service. This includes the Monthly Storage fee, the order handling fee, the Weight Handling and the Pick and Pack service.

1 - Monthly Storage

This is calculated on cubic feet and is charged every calendar month. Do note that the fee changes based on the time of the year, and the cubic foot of storage is more expensive from October to December than the rest of the year.

2 - Order Handling

This is only charged on standard-size non-media items, and it's a 1$ fee. There is no fee on oversized items.

3 - Pick and Pack

This fee is completely based on the size tier of the product, for example, the fee for standard-size units is 1.04$, and it increments as the products move upwards in the size tier.

4 - Weight Handling

This is charged based on the outbound shipping rates, and the amount will depend entirely on the weight of the product.

It is important to note that most of these fees don't get charged on orders that exceed the 300$ mark.

c. Optional Fees

There are a lot of fees on the FBA service that aren't charged on every item processed. The special Handling Fee is a good example of this, as it is a 40$ fee that is only applied to plasma TVs with screens of 42" of larger.

Another optional fees worth mentioning are the Inventory shipping and product preparation services. The first is a service that helps you send your products to an Amazon fulfillment center, while the latter is used if you want to put the task of preparing and labeling your products in the hands of Amazon personnel.

d. The Fee Preview

Amazon never stops working to make your life as a seller easier, and with this purpose, they created a set of tools called Fee Preview. Using these tools you will be able to search and view the estimated fulfillment fees for every product in your inventory.

Do note that the Fee preview only takes into account the core fees that apply to every product. All of the optional services that generate fees won't be included, so the final amount may vary.

Also, keep in mind that this service will only work for products that have dimensions associated with them, so if you haven't entered any dimensions for your products you won't be able to preview your fees.

To see Amazon FBA's latest fee charges, please check **FBA Fulfillment Fees** page.

FBA Fulfillment Fees page: http://goo.gl/wi1d8g

YouTube Video Tutorials
- **How to Accurately Calculate Amazon FBA Fees:** https://goo.gl/eYYGNg
- **Amazon Selling Fees - How to Profit on Amazon AFTER fees:** https://goo.gl/msWJ9f
- **Amazon FBA Fees (Get The Most From Your Money):** https://goo.gl/J2H6Fs
- **NEW Amazon FBA FEE Increase Will Hit Your Business Hard If You Don't Shield Yourself:** https://goo.gl/zc2Y6t
- **How to Avoid Long-Term Storage Fees on Your Amazon FBA Inventory:** https://goo.gl/VLS58x

CHAPTER 7: MANAGING FBA INVENTORY

If you want to stay in a seller relationship with Amazon, you need to make sure that you always have enough inventories on your hands to cover customer demand. However, when using the Fulfillment by Amazon service it may be hard to keep track of this, as the products are no longer in plain sight.

In the "Manage inventory" page there is a suite of tools that allow almost real-time management of your inventories, and it is really important that you learn how to use and squeeze the most out of each one of them.

a. All Inventory View

This is one of the three main pages that you will find in the "Manage inventory" portion of the seller central. You will use this page to create new listings and offer your products on Amazon. In here you will also find all the listings you have created on Amazon.

Once the listing is created, you need to select the box that appears at the left of it and use the "actions" dropdown menu to convert the order processing method to Fulfilled by Amazon. You can also do the same process backwards to change it back to Fulfilled by Merchant in the case you want to handle a particular product.

b. Inventory Amazon Fulfills

In this page, you will find all the information regarding the listings that Amazon fulfills for you. Data like the merchant SKU, the title, condition, price and quantity of your products is displayed on sortable tables.

At the bottom of the screen, you will find four tabs that provide you with a wealth of information related to shipped products. Whether they are inbound (seller to Amazon) or Outbound (Amazon to the customer) you will find all the information you need.

The first tab is the Summary, where you will find the following information.

- **Inbound:** The quantity of every shipment that has not yet been received by Amazon.

- **Fulfillable:** This shows the quantity of products within the network that Amazon will be able to pick, pack and ship.

- **Unfulfillable:** This shows the quantity of products that Amazon has deemed unfit for sale.

- **Reserved:** This refers to your products within the network that are currently tied to an order or are moving between centers.

- **MFN Listing:** If it says "Yes" the item is listed for fulfillment by Merchant.

- **AFN Listing:** A "yes" here indicates Amazon lists the item for fulfillment.

The Second tab is called "Inbound" and it has information regarding all the shipments you have done to an Amazon fulfillment center.

- **Working quantity** refers to shipments you already notified Amazon about.

- **Inbound quantity** is the number of shipments you provided a tracking number for.

- **Receiving quantity** is the number of shipments that already reached the fulfillment center and are being processed.

- **Inbound problem quantity** refers to the items that reached the center but can't be processed due to any reason.

- **Total inbound quantity** is the summary of all the above numbers.

The Outbound tab provides you with information regarding the inventory that has been shipped to a customer. Here you will find the date and type of shipment, quantity of the product and the shipping price.

The last tab is the "Events" tab, where you can check all the events related to your products that Amazon fulfills. It shows you the date the event occurred, the type of event (Receipt, outbound shipment, and adjustment) and the quantity of products involved in the event.

c. The Shipping Queue

On the last part of the Manage Inventory Page, you will find all the information regarding your shipments to Amazon fulfillment centers. It is also the page you use to notify Amazon of your shipments, editing a shipment and deleting or canceling one of them.

The shipment status will tell you where your products stand in the shipping workflow and it is in this screen where you can make most of the actions related to your shipments. Below are the names of the status that you can find on this page.

- **Working**: There is information you haven't inputted yet.

- **Ready to ship:** The information is complete, but you haven't marked the item shipped yet.

- **Shipped:** This means you clicked the "mark as shipped" button for the products.

- **In-Transit:** This only applies to FTL and LTL shipments, and it indicates that there is an appointment made for delivery.

- **Delivered:** The carrier has indicated they delivered the shipment.

- **Checked-In:** The center reported the delivery.

- **Directed to Prep:** The order has been directed to the prep center for the appropriate labeling and preparation.

- **Receiving:** The contents are being scanned and added to your inventory.

- **Closed:** All the contents of your shipment have been processed and are ready for fulfillment.

- **Canceled:** You have canceled the shipment.

- **Deleted:** You have deleted the shipment.

- **Receiving w/ problems:** There were problems found in your shipment.

On this page, you can also edit any shipment that hasn't been received in a fulfillment center. It is possible to set up a notification system that will let you know via e-mail when your products get checked-in. When they are being processed into the inventory of a fulfillment center and when the process is completed.

d. Tools for Managing FBA Inventory

If you find the suite of tools provided by Amazon insufficient to manage your inventories, you may want to try a third party app. There are many of these apps in the market, and you will have to do some research to find the one that suits your needs the best.

1 - Ecomdash
Ecomdash, for example, is a tool that focuses on making it easier for you to manage your inventories across multiple platforms. When it comes to the world of internet selling, your inventory is the most important part of your business, as people who buy online don't want to wait a long time to receive their products.

Most of the tools you will find out there have this focus, to make it easier for you to work on many different platforms and marketplaces.

It is recommended that you invest into one of these tools once your business starts expanding, as you will need a hand to stay organized and make sure you don't disregard any platform you work on.

Ecomdash website:
https://www.ecomdash.com/

2 - Teikametrics

Another useful tool is called **teikametrics**. This app offers a huge amount of information and statistics about sales. It is built to help you maximize your profits on Amazon. You can find graphs on everything, from seasonal trends to the most sold items.

Teikametrics website:
http://www.teikametrics.com/amazon-fba.html

It also helps you make your inventory efficient and profitable. You can track what are the items that sell the most in your inventories, compare the profit made from your items of different brands, you can use this info to prioritize these products and make the most out of your FBA membership.

This tool can also help you take a systematic and efficient approach to stale inventory. One of the disadvantages of FBA is that since you don't see the products all the time you don't really notice if your inventory is going stale. Stale inventory can be a waste of space and it will produce extra FBA fees if it sleeps in storage for too long.

The important part about third party tools is that they need to offer you something you're lacking. Really think about the needs you have as a seller, and if amazon is not giving you all you need to be successful then don't be afraid to look somewhere else to enhance your experience and your profit.

CHAPTER 8: UNDERSTANDING SALES RANK

One of the easiest ways to sell more on Amazon is to raise the ranking of your products. This has a lot of advantages and will increase your sales dramatically, but the most important thing is that you don't have to do anything. If the ranking of your product increases then it will appear higher and have a lot of visibility, which will lead to a lot of new sales without needing you to change anything about the product.

The first step to increasing the rank of your products on Amazon is understanding how the said ranking works. Amazon uses an algorithm to rate each product, this algorithm will take into account how many reviews and sales your product has. The more reviews the higher it will appear in the lists.

The idea behind sales ranking is so that you can determine the popularity of a product at a given time. Amazon has given no indication as to how the algorithm calculates the sales rank per product, but there have been a substantial amount of research and theories that have attempted to debunk the sales rank counting. One theory is that there's a direct correlation between the times it's sold to the ranking. There's no exact time hinted by Amazon as to when the sales rank updates will be modified however.

Sales rank is as dynamic as can be. You will notice that one moment there would be a drop and then the next, the sales rank would skyrocket. Its unpredictability would tell you to focus on the general trend by past ebb and flow of sales rank data. Furthermore, you can't expect to forecast future trends based on current information.

Based on everything mentioned about sales rank, its accuracy isn't, well, accurate. One way to check the precision is through its product reviews. The more the product reviews, the more reliable it is. If you happen to come across a good sales rank with no product review at all then that could be a result of a temporary sale.

A great way to get honest reviews on your product is to give it away. It doesn't mean that you should just give it away for free. Instead, you can use the Seller Central to set-up a discount promotion to buy your product for cheap. Then, give these to your friends and family, or you can do some kind of contest on your website, if you have one, the idea is that people will use the coupon to buy your product and you can ask them to leave a review on the page.

A few facts of sales rank:

- **Sales ranks are only available within particular categories and don't rank the product in the overall Amazon market.** However, there can be subcategories with books, for example having genres with different sales ranks.

- **Each edition of the same product, for example, a book produced in hardcover and kindle, has separate ranking standings.**

- **No sales rank available? This could be the reason:**

  - The product hasn't sold yet on Amazon.

  - Possibly it could have been listed in the miscellaneous category since it's not categorized.

- It could be in a category that doesn't rank, for example, electronics.

- **If there's a cancelation on the purchase, it doesn't affect the sales rank.** It's as if it never happened. However, if there are returns on a product, the original purchase will improve your sales rank. But the return doesn't drop the sales rank at all.

- **Every sales rank is relative to the sale of its rivals.** There's a possibility that your product has plenty of purchases, however, it still loses in sales rank. This is because, in comparison to its competitors, it's not doing well.

- **Funny enough if you haven't sold an item for quite some time, your ranking can still maintain its rank or decrease at a slow rate.** Why? Apparently, if your merchandise consistently sold copies before and then had a dry spell, it could explain that phenomenon.

Since you know the overview of the sales rank idea, here are some qualities of a good sales rank:

- **A publicly accepted good rank is if your rank reaches the top 10%.** Those within the top 1-5% are then considered the fast sellers.

- **Your rank status parallels the season.** If your products are Halloween decorations, you will receive a good sales rank due to high popularity purchases prior to October in comparison to your rank around Easter.

- **A positive rank status could depend on item availability.** If you are the only seller at that moment and you rarely sell an item, you could achieve a higher rank. Due to the fact that there are no other current sellers within that time.

- **If your product sales have been stagnating for a while now, I suggest you inquire about advertising in the Amazon Sponsored Product ads.** It will boost your item's exposure especially in web pages that are more likely able to attract a larger audience.

Since there are so many similar products Amazon had to create an algorithm that will put the items that have the highest chance of selling at the top of the search results. Amazon's main goal is always to maximize Revenue Per Customer. I'll go over the top factors that put items at the top of the list.

1 - Sales Rank

Sales Rank is the number one factor when it comes to ranking on Amazon. There should be no surprise that the items that are selling the most will continue to sell and remain on the top of lists.

2 - Customer Reviews

Next would be Customer Reviews. The more positive reviews compared to negative reviews your product has the more likely it will become a top search result. It is not a matter of how many reviews but how many GOOD reviews your product has.

3 - Image Size and Quality

Image Size and Quality are also a big factor. We are going to want one large and high quality image that will provide the buyer with all the information he visually needs instead of multiple normal sized images. This is because Amazon has a zoom feature that will allow the user to view your image up close so the better the image quality the clearer the buyer can see your image when zoomed in.

4 - Pricing

Pricing is the last factor that I will mention. Amazon understands that customers are always looking for the best deals.

A good deal consists of a good quality product at a low price. If you're product has received positive reviews and has proven to be of good quality then the pricing will be the determining factor when it comes to the Rankings.

To conclude, although you can base how well or poorly your product is doing, try not to consume yourself over the ranks. There are various factors and reasons as to how they come up with the ranks. Other factors such as product reviews, browsing frequency and whether a product is available or not, may or may not directly affect the algorithm. Amazon's sworn oath to secrecy to their sales rank computation has only left you internally debating with yourself. This will make you realize that at the end of the day, you actually have products to sell and a business to take care of.

YouTube Video Tutorials

- **Understanding Sales Rank and Counting Past Sales:** https://goo.gl/kcSC3m
- **Why Amazon Sales Rank Sucks: The Real Tools To Double Your Amazon FBA Sales Right Now:** https://goo.gl/XzagRJ
- **How to do Sales Promotions to boost Rankings with Amazon FBA:** https://goo.gl/hkSMFk
- **How to stay ranked on the first page on Amazon:** https://goo.gl/hfNuVX
- **The Secret Methods to Launch a Product to the Top of the Rankings on Amazon:** https://goo.gl/PSDfbM
- **How to use Sales Rank to Find Products to Sell on Amazon.com:** https://goo.gl/QKrGvn

CHAPTER 9: PACKAGING ITEMS AND SHIPPING INVENTORY

Following the rules required by Amazon for the packaging of your product and preparing the proper inventory labels is a must. The consequences that would follow if you don't adhere to Amazon's prescriptions are the following: refusal of the package at the Amazon fulfillment centers, disposal or return of the product. If breached, it could also possibly lead to future blocking of shipments or additional charges for the further preparation required by FBA or sanctions for its noncompliance. Explained next are attributes of packaging that you should take into consideration:

- **There are essential packaging requirements for individual products.** You will need the specific barcode or label for each unit or set that can be easily detected and identified.

- **For loose products:** Products that consist of more than one component must be parceled into one package. For example, Build-It-Yourself products or a collection of books. Shoes also need to be secured in a box or carton that covers the entire item.

- **Items sold as a set:** You'll need to clearly indicate if the merchandise is to be sold as a separate unit or as a set via a label in the front.

- **Box units:** When packaging it in a box, make sure it has 6 sides with an opening that can easily be identified. If it's effortless to open, make sure that it is shut tight via taping measures.

To decide whether to have additional safety materials on the bag, you can apply a drop test. You'll need to drop it within 3 feet from the ground on each side and one corner. If it clearly open, you'll need extra material to keep it stable. Those additional materials can come in the form of bubble wrap, paper, air pillows and polyethylene foam.

- **Units requiring plastic bags:** Poly bags need to have a suffocation warning somewhere on the package that is comfortably legible for people to understand. This will prevent any lawsuits against you since there was an indicated warning.

  The bag must be transparent which contains a barcode or can allow scanning that passes the plastic. There has to be a seal so you are able to take things and put things in with ease.

- **Understand specific box dimensions, weight, and additional contents.** Guarantee that they follow the guidelines set out by Amazon. For example, a box that contains standard-size shouldn't go beyond 25 inches on each side. Amateur suppliers will make the mistake of using the wrong measurements. So you better read up and commit to memory these minuscule details.

- **The particulars of how to pack a television set** by taking to consideration the pallet, floor loading, and product stacking guidelines.

- **To inventory your products, you'll need to make sure that the labeling specifications are correct** with a valid barcode and information.

- **To ensure an uncomplicated shipment of your merchandise, make sure your shipment labels are properly identified and scannable.**

Previously stated are just customary ways of packaging your items. However, Amazon is rigorous in the packaging process that will require paying attention to the nooks and crannies.

a. Small Products

What are the attributes of a small product? The largest size that is considered "small" is anything below 2-1/8". You can measure your item without the hassle of a measuring instrument via a credit card's length. If it fits within that size, it is considered small. In order to preserve the product and to prevent the product from losing its value caused by external factors, such as dirt or dust, you'll need to package it in a plastic bag. The plastic bag used should be able to cover all areas of the item without any parts of the merchandise protruding. For products that are undeniably tiny, the packing will make it easier to locate them. The plastic has to be transparent with a *suffocation warning* label to prevent civil liberties from complaining if anything goes wrong.

A label with a barcode needs to be clearly presented in the front of the package or any area with a large surface area.

This will allow you or anyone else to scan the barcode without tampering with the already sealed well. This will also prevent any interference between the supplier and the consumer.

One thing you shouldn't do with a small package is to force it into a tiny bag, it will break open the plastic. If your product has sharp corners, it can erode the plastic due to constant handling resulting in the loss or irreversible damage to that object. People also make the mistake of packing it in a dark container. That's a big no as you won't be able to effortlessly identify your item.

b. Apparel, Fabric, Plush, and Textiles

If your item is a type of fabric that can be easily affected gravely by dust or humidity, it is considered a textile, apparel, fabric or plush. These types of merchandise need to be fastened tightly in a poly bag or a shrink-wrap. The purpose is to prevent any destruction of the product during the shipment preparation and process. This is vital since you cannot expect to give less than what the customers are paying for. Textiles are one of the most popular items in the Amazon market and competition is fierce. Focusing on an excellent service will improve ratings and, eventually, profit.

When you **bundle** your products, individual units of fabric or textiles needs to be sealed with a transparent bag or shrink-wrap. You'll need to make sure that it is complete with a *suffocation warning* label to prevent any unnecessary lawsuit just in case the plastics are being misused. Also, labels need to be presented in an area of the package that is easy to scan and swift to detect. When sending shoes, you'll need to package each pair in a box or poly bag with no parts of the shoe exposed to the external factors. You'll need to tape the box shut with non-adhesive band or tape so that the box will also be preserved. You shouldn't pack each shoe separately as it will be difficult and time-costly to locate the other pair constantly. A box would do. Furthermore, don't include hangers in packing. You can ship it independently.

Product Bundling Policy page: https://goo.gl/JLPmRU

c. Fragile Products

You can tell when a product is fragile by its potential to break into smaller pieces at any time between the origin of the product, during shipping and handling, to the end result. This creates a danger to anyone in contact with the item during storage and shipment. Sharp points can also be a concern to other products in storage as it may corrupt their containers. To prevent any risk, you can either pack your product in a protected box or blanket it in bubble wrap to the point where the sharp edges won't harm anyone or anything.

When placing your fragile products in a set, make sure you pack and wrap them up individually. For example, when sending glass memorabilia in a bundle, you'll need to wrap them before you place them within a carton. When placing the objects within a box, use a box with six sturdy surfaces to compress the products and prohibit them from colliding with each other. If you still doubt whether your fragile item is ready for shipment, you can check by applying the 3-foot drop test. With this, you'll need to drop your item five times: on the base, on the top, on the longest side, on the shortest side, and on a corner. You have to be certain that your item will be able to withstand forces going against it. If you leave pockets of empty spaces in the package, it will more likely lead to breakages.

d. Products with Expiration Dates

Food, beverages, and any other items that are sensitive to temperatures are replenishables that have their own rules when it comes to packing and shipping. Since the Amazon storage and shipping transportation don't have climate-controlled environments, it is difficult to make sure they end up safe.

For date-sensitive products, the expiration dates must be visible outside the packaging as well as in each individual unit. Amazon will only accept the price if the shelf life is greater than 90 days from the time of receipt.

As soon as the units reached 50 days, Amazon will remove it for disposal. Therefore, it's a better idea to invest on groceries with a longer shelf life.

For temperature –sensitive products, they must be able to go through 50 degrees minimum temperature and at least a maximum temperature of 100 degrees in the product's shelf life. Chocolates are a tricky item to sell. They can only exist during the colder part of the year and not during hot climates. If you require freezing, refrigeration and air-conditioning, Amazon will not welcome the request, unfortunately.

Other tricky shipments would be potato chips and cookies. The handling does not guarantee that the product will be crumb-free, so it's the supplier's responsibility to pack the product as secure as possible. Before making any supplier decisions with wholesalers and manufacturers, read up on the list of restricted items that Amazon has presented. These are items banned for reselling and distribution due to the hazardous chemicals, for example, nail polish.

e. Baby Products

Baby products consist of items that are used solely by children who are three years of age or younger. Also, the item must be greater than 1"x1" so that there won't be any wear and tear of the product during the shipment, any form of preparation and stocking in the Amazon storage.

You can either place the merchandise in a six-sided package or place it in a sealed plastic bag or shrink-wrapped. For example, pacifiers in bundles are able to fit soundly within a box. However, a medium to large toys that come in all shapes and sizes shouldn't be placed in a box. You'll be using up your time and money when you can easily fit the toy in a poly bag. If it's fragile, however, you should pack it accordingly to the tips in Part B.

You need to validate that the suffocation warning labels are clearly written out and aren't creased throughout the packaging. It is a hassle for the Amazon staff to work out problems that arise in the storage when you yourself could have gone a bit further to prevent these difficulties. Since these products are mainly for infants, it is highly likely that the plastics will be within reach of little children. A missing label would prove disastrous due to the fact that a label will be submitted as proof that you have specifically warned the shopper of the misapplication of the packaging. Whatever happens after you've sent the package is in their jurisdiction and not yours.

f. Sharp Products

Products with sharpened points and edges have the ability to harm anyone and anything when being uncovered. This is a safety concern for the staff working at Amazon, the people handling the product, as well as the customers getting and opening the product. You'll need to make sure that you've used the allowed materials to execute the packing for example bubble wrap.

Sharp objects most often than not have a specific container called the blister pack. These packs must be placed in the sharp edges and must be fastened to the product to stop it from sliding around. For example, if you're selling knives in the market, you'll be foolish to just wrap it with one rotation. A couple of layers would be feasible. Packing them individually would be ideal. If you're worried about wrapping bigger and sharper knives, you can add more material or you can even use types of cloth.

Things you shouldn't do are to pack the sharp products in an unsafe-molded footprint. Also, refrain from using cardboard or plastic covering. However, if the plastic is durable and firm and promises no breakages, it's good to go. Sharp objects have the most attention when it comes to shipping and storing the products. If a sharp object gets breaks free, it would lead to a negative outcome in the form of casualties and wounds with the Amazon personnel. Things like that will be prevented when ensuring your product is packed with the utmost care and attention.

g. Collectible Games

When it comes to selling secondhand board games online, first you will need to make sure that all the pieces are complete. If there is indeed something that you are missing at the moment, don't fret. There are usually sites online that are selling individual pieces of the game and just like pieces of a puzzle, you can put them together.

Be ready to splurge a bit on refurbishing the products because it would ultimately be more appealing to the customer as a complete set. However, you'll need to price the product properly since there might be a case where the money you spent on to recondition the product is higher priced than the actual price. Also, make sure that there aren't any signs of wear. Time will also be needed to bring back what it looks like to the closest possible result.

If you've collected games from yard sales and thrift stores, you'll need to clean it thoroughly to make it pleasant for reselling. There are various ways to rehabilitate board games, for example, stickers that damage the box, you can use a hair dryer on low to loosen the adhesive and then just use your fingernails to remove the unwanted sticker. You should organize all the parts into bundles, for example, all the cards into a rubber band. However, if you feel that it may ultimately be the one ruining it, then just leave them loose. Plastic wrapping is perfect, as it won't ruin the print on the boxes.

h. Books for Shipping to Amazon FBA Warehouses

Prioritizing your customers is a must in the Amazon business and packaging books for shipping is no different. If you were in their position and you see a product broken and tattered, it would most probably make your blood boil. Not a pleasant sight. Product presentation at the end result would create a domino effect of positive return.

For one, you may receive good reviews about your product and about you as a supplier in general. This could lead to one of many things: recommendations of your product to their friends, relatives and companions and/or they will become future clients due to your service and reliability. As a moral standpoint, you will feel satisfied that you've provided the commodity that they've fully paid for.

If you produce items in a haphazard fashion unintentionally to meet up with the shipping deadlines, you need to reassess your business structure. If you're too busy or you have just too many orders to fulfill, you can take the option of hiring additional hands. Otherwise, consider reducing your product promotions or amount of products for sale to guarantee a decent experience for your customers.

You'll need to follow these tips to make sure that your product stays safe:

- **Determine the ability of your product to withstand external forces and various weather conditions.**

- **Apply a bag with a perfect fit.** Excess plastic needs to be cut off completely.

- **Proper labeling.** Labels are important to prevent liability in the future. Also, you'll need to make sure that the labels aren't creased, covered or hard to locate.

- **Don't overuse the bubble wrap to secure its safety one layer is suitable.** But if it's still unsafe, use a box.

YouTube Video Tutorials
- **Shipping to Amazon FBA:** https://goo.gl/32pm5B
- **Amazon FBA Rules, Guidelines, and Supplies:** https://goo.gl/9eEP2V
- **Packaging Video Games For Amazon FBA:** https://goo.gl/3Pvp2u
- **How To Make Quick Easy Packing Lists for Amazon FBA Without the Extra Hassle:** https://goo.gl/GKHBNP

CHAPTER 10: PROVIDING CUSTOMER SATISFACTION

When it comes to business, there's always the golden rule: "The customer is always right". Few things measure the success of your business quite as well as customer satisfaction.

No matter what your products are, you should always aim for the complete satisfaction of your customer needs. They are the heart of every business, and how much they want to come back to you is a really good measure of your success.

When it comes to internet business this is especially important, the amount of options a customer has when buying online is immense, and if he is dissatisfied with your service, then there is absolutely no reason for him to shop from you again.

a. The Importance of Customer Satisfaction

Every single business will thrive if its customers are satisfied. There are different levels of satisfaction, and market experts everywhere use these as a metric of how successful a business is. Rating your customer level of satisfaction from one to ten, you can measure the impact they will have on the success of your business.

It is a good idea to see customer ratings to identify the ones who are satisfied and the ones who have issues. To know what they think about the product, use this rating scale from 1 to 5 to analyze the results to see what needs to improve.

5 Star:
Customers in this level will be so satisfied with your products and services that they will become you best tool of marketing. Not only they will say great things about your products to their social circle, they will also fight for your product if anyone is saying bad things about it.

4 Star:

Customers in this level are satisfied with your service, but they still think you can do better. You should focus your efforts on this group, identify the things you could have done to better satisfy their needs and apply what you learn to other customers.

3 Star or Below:

This level of satisfaction in unacceptable. Customers won't come back to a business they are this dissatisfied with. Read their reviews then apply what you learn from these reviews.

Customer satisfaction is especially important if you want to have a great success as a seller on amazon, for two main reasons.

1 - Amazon and Its Customers

The first reason to put customer satisfaction at the top of your list is that Amazon cares a lot about their customers. The image they want to project is the one of a company that puts the satisfaction of their users first. They also expect that you, as a seller, help them succeed at this.

The satisfaction of your Customers plays a huge role in your ranking as a seller in Amazon, so you need to ensure you put the customer first if you want your listings to have high visibility.

Don't think of this as a chore thought, satisfying your customers' needs will increase your profitability and is one of the best things to invest your time and money on.

2 - Customer Loyalty

The second reason comes from a problem that has existed since online shopping was conceived: a problem with customer loyalty. The success of a business will always be tied to how reliably you can get customers to buy from you again every time.

b. Buyer-Seller Messaging Service

What the *Buyer-Seller Messaging Service* permits you as a seller is to communicate with Amazon buyers in their marketplace through the use of e-mail. You have the ability to review emails that have been sent to and from buyers that can be found in the **Buyer-Seller Messages page**. In order to see this, go to your **seller account home page** and check Buyer Messages within the Performance box.

Buyer-Seller Messages page: http://goo.gl/ypTGF4
Seller account home page: http://goo.gl/srSyug

Usually, buyers have questions they want to ask personally to their sellers about the product they're purchasing. Fulfillment by Amazon fulfills this need through the Buyer-Seller Messaging Service, although, Amazon will still be handling some of your inquiries on behalf of the sellers.

If you want to use this feature, consider enabling the service through your personal account. When fulfilling your own orders, using the Buyer-Seller Messaging Service will be enabled by default and then you can facilitate buyer service requests.

Allowing Questions on Products for FBA orders

By answering buyer's product questions using the Buyer-Seller Messaging Service could prove to improve your buyer's experience. When you explain to them in-depth of your product knowledge, you will potentially reduce any returns from customers and increase repeat purchases.

If you want to enable Buyer-Seller Messaging Services so that the buyers send you inquiries about your products, then follow these steps:

> 1. Click Settings drop-down menu, select Fulfillment by Amazon
>
> 2. Go to Product Support and click Edit button
>
> 3. Select Enable
>
> 4. Update It

Warning: the Buyer-Seller Messaging Service is for product inquiries only. Anything related to customer service on any Amazon-fulfilled orders should be directed to Amazon Customer Service.

1. Advantages of Buyer-Seller Messaging

Here are the following benefits of using the Buyer-Seller Messaging Service:

- Increased security of Buyer-Seller communication, due to masks on private email addresses

- Both buyers and sellers can see emails from the service and from the companies email system, such as Gmail, Yahoo, Outlook, etc.

- It is encouraged as a way to reduce disputes and claims

- In the case of disputes or claim, Amazon could assist with ease due to its accessibility to corresponding between the sellers and buyers

- Encrypted Alias' are provided when using Buyer-Seller Messaging Services between both buyers and sellers. For example: if a seller wants to inquire to the buyer, Buyer-Seller Messaging Service will display 'dshrn239@marketplace.amazon.com' instead of the supposed email.

What the Buyer-Seller Messaging Service does is provide a record of an email through Amazon's systems, finding it easier to reply or to contact to either buyer or seller through the use of your personal or business e-mailing system. You can do this and the service will still record your correspondence using an encrypted alias.

Keep in mind that not every message you receive is expected a response. When you check the '*mark as no response needed*' box in the reply section of the communication thread, it will shut out the message from any **contact response time performance metrics**. You can use this when the conversation has reached its end or to send a '*out of the office*' message to buyers.

Contact Response Time Metrics page:
http://goo.gl/5m4T9k

Be warned that when you have set your listings to inactive, for when you go to vacations or other absence matters that it does not necessarily inactivate your Buyer-Seller Messaging Service. There will still be a contact response time expected of you while listed as inactive.

When Answering your Buyer

You can choose to directly send your personal or business email systems with your encrypted email address that is generated by the Buyer-Seller Messaging Service. Make sure to treat this encrypted email address like you would any other. Once the email has reached Amazon's systems, it will be visible in the '*Sent Messages*' within the Buyer-Seller page. Even when the sending of messages to Amazon is delayed, it will show in Amazon's system.

2. Guidelines

Basically, what the Buyer-Seller Messaging Services provide for you is a platform for you to contact Amazon.com customers to complete orders or to respond to inquiries only. Any other form of contact with buyers, for marketing or promotional purposes, that includes media forms such as email, physical mail, or otherwise, is not allowed.

If ever you want the option of enabling or blocking access by your company's employees to your seller account, you could go see the Using the **Alternative Address Feature.**

Alternative Address Feature: http://goo.gl/RdgMZt

When you send any permitted email to an Amazon.com customer, your email should **not** include any of the following:

- Links to any website

- Seller logos that may contain a link to the seller's website

- Marketing messages or promotional advances

- Promotion for additional products or referrals to any other third party products

Contact Methods

Steps when wanting to contact a buyer with your seller account:

1. Look for **Manage Orders**, locating the order that you want to contact the buyer

2. Name of the buyer in '*Contact Buyer*'

3. Next page, enter the message you would like to send to that specified buyer

4. Click Submit when finalized.

Manage Orders page: https://goo.gl/yjCytN

Steps when wanting to contact a buyer using your personal or business account:

1. Got to **Manage Orders**, locate order that you want to contact the buyer

2. Name of buyer in *'Contact Buyer'*

3. Copy encrypted email address that is seen next to the buyer's name in the *'To'* area of the page

4. Go to your email and paste the copied email address to contact the buyer. (Be advised that the buyer will not see your email as it would be passing the Amazon Messaging Service to encrypt your email for you)

Searching and Filtering your Messages
You are given several different filter options that are available when you send and receive messages, here are your options:

- **Searching**
  When looking at the search box on top of the page, you can search for messages that may be linked to a specific ID or ASIN. You are also able to search for messages that have been sent and received to and from a specific email address. Keep in mind that this does not regard the body of the mail.

- **Filter Options**
  Click *'Show Filter Options'* that is shown at the top of the page. Filter your messages by date, response status or attachment status.

  When you filter by date, you are given the option to pre-define the time frame or place an exact date

When you filter by response status, you can select messages that have yet to be responded or messages that may have received a response within a pre-defined time frame.

When you filter by attachment status, you can only see messages that have placed attachments within them

E-mail Templates

If you are a seller, I am sure that you would receive more than a handful of messages that you may frequently have to reply to. Sometimes, these messages may seem like you are sending the same response. To prevent from having to constantly be writing down the same messages, you can create templates for the messages you commonly send buyers.

For further information on this feature, check **E-mail Templates.**

E-mail Templates page: http://goo.gl/Sg57yk

Attachments

When sending messages, you can send more than one attachment to the buyer. You also have the option to receive attachments from your buyers.

You will know that there is an attachment on a file when there is a paper clip icon that is seen on the right of the subject field within the Buyer-Seller Messages.

Take note that the allowed attachment size is 10MB max.

Here are the following document formats that the messaging service supports:
- Text files (.txt)
- PDF (Portable Document Format)
- Word Files (.doc or .docx)
- Image Files (.jpg, .gif, .tiff, .bmp or .png)

Warning: Amazon has the authority to remove any content that is deemed inappropriate

Customer Response Time Metrics

What is the response time on Amazon?

Well, it is a measure of the percentage of customer initiated messages that you are required to respond to within 24 hours.

Amazon wants to make sure that you are sending high-quality and fast responses to the customer's inquiries because they are an important factor when dealing with customer satisfaction. Of course, Amazon has a high customer satisfaction rate.

Amazon's research shows that those who send messages back to their buyers within the 24 hours have a 50% less chance of getting a bad review compared to those who have received a response after 24 hours.

For more detail on this subject, including how customer metrics are used in Amazon to evaluate your seller account then see the **Understand Customer Metrics** page.

Customer Metrics page: http://goo.gl/aQ9YY4

c. Working Towards Customer Satisfaction

No business can exist without customers, and no customer will want to keep making business with a service they are dissatisfied with. It is important that you make customer satisfaction your number one goal, and every single action you take on your business has to be focused towards that goal.

Remember that as an Amazon seller, you are competing with thousands of other merchants who are often offering the same products you have. A satisfied customer base will raise your rank as a seller on the site, and this is the only way you will differentiate from the rest.

1 - Give it the Time That it Deserves
A lot of online businesses fail when it comes to customer satisfaction because they are not willing to put in the effort and the time it takes to become good at it. It takes a lot of time and studying to become good at providing satisfaction.

You need to constantly study the market and the customer base you are targeting. If you target public is comprised of young adults you will handle them a lot different that if you offer products for the elderly.

Get to know your customers and learn about their particular needs. No customer is the same and there isn't a way to satisfy everyone.

Don't get stuck in the mentality of "I don't need to change" because times change. If you made the jump from a traditional business to an internet shop, und that the way you approach customer satisfaction will also change.

2 - Go the extra mile

Customers, especially those that are used to shop on amazon, will normally have a lot of expectations of what the seller will do for them. A great part of customer satisfaction comes from exceeding these expectations. If customers send you some questions about your products, answer them promptly and politely.

Put yourself in the place of the buyer and think about what you would expect from a seller. Make sure you go the extra mile for your customers. Let them know how much you care and consistently show them why you're different from the other sellers.

a. Ways to Improve Customer Satisfaction

Now that you recognize how important customer satisfaction is for any business, it is time to think about what you can do to keep your customers happy. Your internet business faces very specific challenges that don't exist on a typical business, especially when it comes to building a relationship with your customers.

Due to the nature of Amazon and the way it shows every potential buyer hundreds of choices for every product, it can be really hard to build a customer base that will stay loyal. But only because you work over the internet it doesn't mean that your business is bound to never have a loyal customer base. Customer satisfaction is the way you make sure you get loyal customers.

1 - Surprise your Customer

When you sell your products online, a big portion of your sales will come from people who buy on impulse. A big question that often pops into the minds of these people right after they've done paying is "what's that worth it?" You definitely don't want your customers to ask themselves this, as it paints your service in a negative light from the beginning.

A great way to avoid this is by providing a little bonus with every purchase. You can do this through **bundling**. It can be anything, and it doesn't need to be expensive.

The point is that the surprise of receiving something unexpected will make your customers feel better and secure about the purchase they just made.

If your product requires any kind of training to be used effectively, a great way to give your customer a bonus is to offer them free online support on the product they just purchased by putting up training videos on your product website. *If you used a private label or EOM to manufacture your products, then you can ask your manufacturer to include your website in your product packaging labels and instruction manuals.* They will feel you care about them and it reduces the chance of them getting frustrated with the product, which would lead to bad reviews.

To do this, you should create a website for all your products that can provide a

2 - The Customer as a Mirror

The first and most important rule when it comes to customer service is that you should treat them like you would want to be treated. This philosophy is the single best approach to Customer services at it has many advantages.

When you put yourself at the same level as your customers like this, you are most likely to give them the answers they are looking for.

Constantly ask your customer questions that help you understand their point of view, and make the effort to think about what you would like to hear if you were in their position.

3 - Yes, Yes and Yes

It's no coincidence that the first thing you learn about customer service is that "The customer is always right". When dealing with your customers, the word "No" should be out of your vocabulary. You should answer everything they say with words that show you agree with them.

However, this doesn't mean that you should answer every single inquiry with a yes, and it is very important that you don't make promises that you won't be able to fulfill just to avoid a confrontation with the customer. This is a very common mistake that sellers make all the time. What is really important is that your customer feels that you are on his side at all times.

When you are forced to give a negative answer on anything, make sure you avoid downright saying no. It is better if you first apologize, tell them that you understand the reasons they have to make such a request, but that is not possible to fulfill it at the time being.

If you give your client a good explanation of the reason of your negative, they are less likely to fight with you.

Also, make sure you offer an alternative after your negative, so you steer the conversation away from the "no" and show them you are trying your best to provide solutions.

4 - Get to Know your Product

This doesn't apply to every kind of product, but if you are selling something you should be an expert in EVERYTHING related to the product. People will make every kind of weird questions, and it is important that you can answer all of them without doubting for a second.

You should also study and learn about the shipping process, how Amazon works, and everything that you think a customer might ask. You might be good with computers, but a 60-year-old grandma might make her first Amazon buy with you and she will have a lot of questions that she will expect you to answer.

5 - Leave the Script to the Theater

It is recommended that you don't write any scripts to answer customer inquiries. Your conversations with customers should feel personal and not robotic. Also, getting used to working with a script is a terrible habit that will make your Customer service fail in the long run.

6 - Resolving Customer Issues

Customer service includes many things, but the main one is about resolving any issues your buyers may have with your products. In your Amazon online business, this will often include problems with the shipments, and technical support if your products have anything to do with technology.

b. Steps To Solve Customer's Problem

Customer Service is not only about solving problems. It is about solving them efficiently. Time is limited, and oftentimes it will be only you working to solve many different issues at the same time. Follow these steps to keep your problem solving as efficient as possible and you will be able to provide your Customers with the service they deserve.

Step #1 - Be Thankful

The first thing you should do is thanking the customer for taking the time to reach for you to complain, it will show them that you value their time and ideas.

Step #2 - Be sorry

Tell your Customer that you are sorry he's having a hard time. It shows sincerity and sympathy on your side.

Step #3 - Find The Real Problem

Customers may use this time to say a lot of things that surround the problem and that's information that you don't need. Focus on the central issue the customer is having and work from there to try and find a solution.

Step #4 - Find a Solution

Start working immediately in finding a solution for the problem the customer brought to your attention. You can even discuss ideas, including him in the process until you reach agreement on a solution.

Step #5 - Say Thank You Again

After you are done explaining the solution to the customer and their issue is (hopefully) a thing of the past, don't forget to thank them for contacting and assure them they can contact you any time if another issue pops up. A good customer service can get you far and someone who receives good attention will tell his or her friends about it. It is the best word of mouth you can have.

Although most of the issues your customers will ask for help with have to do with shipment or problems of usage of your products, every once in a while you will get a message from a customer just because he wants to give you a complaint about your product or service.

A big problem a lot of sellers have is that they don't know how to take the critic and will answer with hostility toward the customer. "Who does he think he is?" is the first thing that comes to their mind when in reality, they should be thankful that someone is taking the time to tell him what he could do to improve his business.

The customer may not always be right, but he is still the central piece in any business, and he or she is always the customer we need.
When you receive a complaint, make sure the customer feel he is being heard and taken into account. And for your part as a seller, make sure you learn something from the experience and make your business better from these complaints.

CHAPTER 11: EXPANDING YOUR BUSINESS

Whether you are either a new seller in the market and want to sell internationally or even an already established experienced international seller, the use of Amazon Global Selling is a perfect platform into the direction of growing your business.

Amazon has constantly been growing its marketplace and they have marketplaces all over the world – United States, Canada, Spain, United Kingdom, Germany, France, Italy, China, Japan and even in India. Apart from their international marketplace, Amazon has the variety of services and tools that you may need in creating a successful global marketplace.

When listing your items in Amazon's marketplace, you instantly provide access to millions of customers that are located worldwide.

In this chapter, you will be able to find an overview of the things that you will need as you attempt to expand your business in an international scale – with the use of Amazon.

Here are step-by-step instructions; how-to guides and the tools that will help you get going as an international Amazon seller.

STEP #1: Understand How Selling Globally on Amazon Works

Before engaging in your online sales to international customers, be sure to understand your business. Being able to understand what and where to sell gives you the startup information about how you will sell globally with Amazon.

Amazon sells in ten different marketplaces around the world.

- North America (United States and Canada)

- Europe (United Kingdom, France, Italy, Germany and Spain)

- Asia (Japan, China and India)

Before selecting an area to sell, make sure you understand whether or not your product is appropriate for the country. This may refer to the different laws they require for each country, product standards and the local language.

STEP #2: Various Taxes and Regulations

Now that you may have established an area where you will be selling, you need to be able to understand the tax and regulations that country has. Every country has different legal and industrial requirements that concern the subject of sales of products to the consumers.

Make sure you research on the regulations of the area you consider selling to. These are some of the things to consider:

- Tax and Customs

- Intellectual Property Rights

- Parallel Importation

- Export Controls

- Markings and Labels

- Environment, Health and Safety

- Product Obedience

STEP #3: Structure Your Account and Begin

This step journeys into setting up your Seller Central account in the selected Amazon marketplace that you have chosen and then creating the different product offers to start selling.

Even if you have an account for the Amazon marketplace you are selling in, you have to create another one for your chosen area.

For example, if you sell in China and you want to sell in France, you will need to create a new Amazon seller account in their provided Amazon websites. The only exception is that if you have created an account in Europe, France and want to sell in Germany, then you can use your same account.

STEP #4: Your Chosen Fulfillment Strategy

Being able to promptly deliver your products to your customers is an important part for an online business and for their customer experience.

In choosing your Fulfillment Strategy, you may choose between fulfilling on your own or use the Fulfillment by Amazon.

STEP #5: Supply Customer Support

Your decision on fulfillment method used for your online marketplace will determine how you will handle your customer support or handle returns.

a. How to Build your Own Multi-Sales Channel?

There is another feature that you can obtain through the use of Fulfillment by Amazon (FBA) this feature is **Multi-Channel Fulfillment**. This feature will enable you as the seller to obtain the same fast, trusted Amazon shipping and fulfillment of all your orders that is made through other sales channels; other than through Amazon.

Multi-Channel Fulfillment page: http://goo.gl/lQx4e8

Be able as a seller to give your customers the fast-shipment experience that Amazon has provided and that they love, this will continuously build your loyal customer base and increase sales.

Does this interest you? If so, this is how it works:

- A single pool of the product inventory of your choosing will be placed in a fulfillment center of Amazon.

- When an order is placed either on Amazon, your own site or any of the other online market platforms.

- Amazon will be the ones to pick, pack and ship it to the customers that have placed the order.

Amazon's fulfillment centers will be the ones to handle most of your inventory requirements and can scale the items to your customer's needs. Amazon will be the ones that handle the details of the order and will allow you to save time and be able to focus more on the business at hand.

1 - Be in-charge of E-Commerce more efficiently with Multi-Channel Fulfillment

Usually, it becomes time-consuming when you have to manage and fulfill all the orders across different channels at one time. It becomes time-consuming, complex and it becomes an addition to your operational costs.

With Multi-Channel Fulfillment enables you the scale of Amazon's world-class and high-ranking fulfillment networks. You can fill orders directly from your own third-party e-commerce site. Doing this lowers your costs dramatically and frees up your time and resources for you to be able to grow your business.

2 - Increased Efficiency with the Use of Multi-Channel Fulfillment

The Multi-Channel Fulfillment entitles you to be capable of easily scaling and managing peak deliveries during the busy times of the year while being able to manage your operational costs.

You maintain the control over customer services and you will have the option to whether you will have returns shipped directly to Amazon fulfillment centers and placed back into your pool inventory where it once was before. Throughout the whole process, you are entitled to retain ownership of the inventory you have placed in the Amazon fulfillment center inventory pool and can request to return the items at any time.

3 - Put Forward Reliable On-Day, Two-Day, and Standard delivery

Do you want to satisfy your customers and make them happy?

With Multi-Channel Fulfillment, you can provide your customers will excellent shipping. Customers want flexible methods of delivery, Multi-Channel fulfillment's are cost-effective and obtain options of one-day or two-day alternative delivery methods that you can offer to your customers partially or fully charging them for whichever option is chosen.

Alternatives for cost-conscious customers are the standard three to five day delivery is available as well.

4 - Cost-Effective and Straightforward

You will be charged for storage space and the orders that will be fulfilled by Amazon but in the long run, you will gain more because it's cheaper and you will have a faster delivery service for all your products to your customers.

YouTube Video Tutorials

- **Amazon FBA Multi-Channel Fulfillment - How To Tutorial:** https://goo.gl/tuuxeE
- **How to Create a Multi-channel Fulfillment Order on Amazon FBA:** https://goo.gl/WFnsW3
- **Multi-Channel Fulfillment For E-commerce, Private Label Or Amazon FBA:** https://goo.gl/3pd2F3
- **How to Create a Multichannel Fulfilled Order on Amazon:** https://goo.gl/BxZzKm

b. How to Drive Product Demand

Now that you have started selling with Amazon and maximizing your use of the benefits that FBA provides, you may be wondering what you can do in order to generate more income and demand for the products that you provide.

In this section, I will discuss some self-service tools from Amazon that will be able to aid you in your search for more customers in order to generate more sales.

The following will explain how to help drive the demand for your products with FBA exports, promotions, advertising and different and new product opportunities.

1 - Grow your Business Internationally

Once you have signed your business up for **FBA export**, Amazon will allow you to reach more international customers and Amazon will show you which products are eligible for international export that you can sell to your customers for a specific region.

FBA Export page: http://goo.gl/G8NdVY

With the use of FBA exports, Amazon will be the one to handle the exporting process and be the one to ship your exportable products to your international customers with no additional costs. Selling to customers all over the world will increase your knowledge on the international demand for your products before you decide to invest your resources into setting up your business within that country.

2 - Promote and Advertise to Your Amazon Customers

Seller Central allows you as a seller to set up your own personal promotions.
A promotion is a useful and great way to provide support for the demand you need and gain visibility of your products in the eyes of the customer.

To gain this advantage, you simply go to the **Advertising** link then click **Manage Promotions** to proceed in creating your own promotions. Here are the steps in creating your own promotions:

> **STEP #1:** Select the various keywords that relate to your products that you want to advertise.

> **STEP #2:** When the shoppers place on of your keywords on Amazon.com, you have a higher chance of your products to be displayed.

> **STEP #3**: Once the keywords are placed, your products are displayed as one of the search items.

> **STEP #4:** Customers who instantly click on your ad will go directly to the page for your listing.

Tip: Your ad will only be displayed for customers once you have offered a competitive bid for your product and your offer has been listed in the Buy Box

The following describes the various types of promotions that your product is entitled to:

- **Money Off**: This means that for each and every item(s) purchased, you will be able to provide the customer a discount.

- **Buy One, Take One**: This is what the title says, for each item purchased, customers can purchase an identical item with no fee.

- **External Benefits**: You can provide your customers a post-order benefit. These benefits provide customers a discount on their future purchase.

3 - Increase Your Product Portfolio

Strategically Increase your FBA Listings: Amazon Selling Coach is a platform that Amazon provides for the sellers in order to aid them with new selling techniques and opportunities with products that may be similar to yours.

Amazon Selling Coach page:
https://goo.gl/fnM4WC

You are able to see your fulfillment, inventory and the opportunities that your products obtain anytime with the use of Amazon Selling Coach dashboard. You can take advantage of this opportunity by selling the products that have been suggested on Amazon.

YouTube Video Tutorials
- **Amazon Coupon Code Video Tutorial - Amazon Promotions:** https://goo.gl/HFUmPv

- **How To Set Up Amazon FBA Promotions: Sell More FBA Items:** https://goo.gl/z7Gckf
- **How To Create One-time Promo Codes in Amazon:** https://goo.gl/cVFYaN

c. How to Brand Yourself?

1 - Brand Neutral Box

This provides you an option to have each of your entitled Multi-Channel Fulfillment shipment packaged in a non-branded box when enabling this service.

- Every entitled Multi-Channel Fulfillment shipment will be billed an extra amount; this fee is $1.00 for every shipment for this service provided and will be added to the per-order fulfillment fees. Any other fees such as Amazon.com Fulfillment shipments and related FBA will not be impacted.

- Your products that are already placed in FBA inventory within the fulfillment centers that are chosen to support by the Brand Neutral service are the ones that will be shipping with non-branded boxes, while the rest of your existing inventory that is not supported by the Brand Neutral service will be shipped with the Amazon-branded boxes.

- Amazon will be the ones to determine which products are eligible to quality for their Brand Neutral service and which will not.

- The moment that you and your products are enabled, the entitled inbound shipments would directly end up in the fulfillment centers that support the Brand Neutral Service

- If one or a group of your product happens to be restricted to a certain fulfillment center that ends up not supporting the Brand Neutral service, will notify you during the process of the inbound shipment creation process.

- You are given the option of whether you would want to disable the Brand Neutral service at any time.

- Amazon may choose to discontinue this feature and proceed to ship all products with an Amazon-branded box when they please.

If you are interested in this method of service and either wish to disable or enable this, go to the Multi-Channel Fulfillment settings that can be found in the Fulfillment by Amazon Settings page.

2 - Packaging Slip Branding

- ### *Merchant Name*

As a seller, you can decide how you want your merchant name to appear on every of our Multi-Channel Fulfillment packing slips. The merchant name is the name that you will use in order to identify yourself for all of your Multi-Channel Fulfillment shipments.

When you enable this service you:

- Will provide displays that would be shown on the upper left corner of every packing slip that is processed through shipping as well as the shipping address of the customer.

- Will gain the option of whether to disable this type of feature at any given point. Once disabled, the space where the merchant name is placed will become blank

Tip: This service provided by Amazon is still in its beta phase. At the moment, there is no charge for this feature, although, Amazon reserves the right to charge the seller for this in the future at any given time.

- ### *Informational Text*

You are able to choose whether you want to add informational text to appear on every Multi-Channel Fulfillment packing slip. This informational slip provided is in addition to the distinctive content you apply to each of your packing slips when your Multi-Channel Fulfillment orders are put forward for fulfillment.

d. Advertising Your Products

Advertising is important for every business in the world. It is not a coincidence that is the one thing that costs the most in the production of every product.
Fortunately for you, one of the advantages of an internet business is that you don't need to spend millions of dollars on advertising and it is really easy to do everything by yourself.

In this era of connection, social media has made it extremely easy to advertise by yourself. Create Facebook, Twitter and Instagram profiles of your products and your amazon Seller profile. It doesn't take a lot of time and it is really easy to maintain them updated.

Make sure you put links to your products on these pages. For people visiting it will be easier to buy something they like if they can see the link at all times. You can also use these sites to offer promotions, which will lead to even more sales.

Amazon Ads

Amazon also has a **system** in place to help you advertise, and it is smart to use it to the fullest. After you set it up it will show ads of your product to potential buyers that are browsing Amazon.

Amazon Ads page: http://goo.gl/Xp2wVZ

You can set up **Amazon Ads** to target certain groups of Amazon shoppers and set a specific time for the promotion. It can also provide you with a report to help you track and improve your advertising campaigns. You can see which keywords led to most sales and set up the ads to target people who search for those keywords.

YouTube Video Tutorials
- **What is Amazon Product Ads?:**
  https://goo.gl/YZZfFR

- **Getting Started with Product Display Ads:**
  https://goo.gl/wMB4Mr
- **Getting Started with Sponsored Products:**
  https://goo.gl/L4WTMC
- **Getting Started with Headline Search Ads:**
  https://goo.gl/sDQYfa
- **How To Use Facebook Ads In Your Amazon Business:** https://goo.gl/uikTnp
- **What is Amazon Pay Per Click PPC Advertising?:**
  https://goo.gl/s3bBbF
- **How To Sell Things On The Amazon Marketplace Using Advertising:** https://goo.gl/cs92BW
- **Solving the Amazon Product Ads Puzzle:**
  https://goo.gl/sHC2Rh

CHAPTER 12: CUSTOMER REVIEWS

Customer reviews are feedbacks made by customers who have bought a product or availed the services they purchased. If they have positive reviews, they would praise the suppliers with their ability to secure a well-maintained shipment of the item from supplier to consumer. However, often than not, feedback would come in the form of unfavorable comments. If a customer shows dissatisfaction in the packaging and/or handling of the product, they would provide a negative opinion. In the best-case scenario, they would provide both advantages and disadvantages, together with suggestions for future deals.

In the worst case scenario, though there will be grave comments with tips directed to other consumers not to purchase your products. But if you've followed religiously the guidelines and rules within this book and regulations demanded by Amazon, then this wouldn't be a problem.

When it comes to authenticating the reviews, it's difficult to fully test their legitimacy. You won't know whether the suppliers have hired themselves to provide good reviews or they've been hired by competitors to downgrade the reviews. The reviews could also be ranked based on their practicality by other users through liking or disliking the reviews. Amazon has devised a way to find out scammers and other false accounts making irrelevant messages all over the Amazon market. But there are still plenty of loopholes and trust is a very uncertain feature in the modern age.

Sarcasm can also be used to attract customers. There are people who provide ironic and sarcastic feedback to produce reviews that are normally seen as tedious and uninteresting. This can be a marketing strategy for you to take advantage of. You can have the most mundane and preposterous item in the world but can still book sales just by the hilarity of the reviews and their popularity. This will attract people since they're curious as to what the fuss is all about. This kind of satire will further add to the amount of people viewing your product. Who knows, maybe you'll get a purchase after all and having a crazy comment will benefit you at the end.

a. How To Get 5 Star Rating And Positive Reviews?

If you believe that selling your items without the need for positive reviews will help you out, then go ahead. Try selling your product in the same market with other fierce competitors without the trust and assurance you give to your customers. A detailed description and a constant use of persuasive language can only do so much. It is one-sided and biased. Imagine hundreds of customers surfing through Amazon and they're stuck between your product and someone else's. The lack of reviews could have you possibly lose hundreds of clients. People are, by nature, indecisive. They function with a cost-benefit analysis embedded in their decision-making process. We humans prefer the comfort of other people and safety in numbers. They'll need to assess your product's reliability based on other people's personal opinion after purchasing your product. Fundamentally, positive reviews seal the deal for hesitant consumers.

How to get a great customer review? First of all, no matter how much effort you put into your work, it is nearly impossible to make EVERYONE give you a 5-star rating. The closer you are, the better. Don't be discouraged with a couple of bad reviews; just make sure they are anomalies to the overall trend. Perhaps you put the wrong labels or miss pack the products. The most common case of negative feedback is when suppliers fail to describe their product with utmost detail. One error even in the tiniest detail can be a nuisance. Even getting the color or the size wrong is a terror. Try to make up for the bad reviews by having loads of good ones.

Sometimes you will come across a customer absolutely adoring your product but would either forget to write a feedback or don't really know the mechanics of writing a review. Usually, Amazon is preprogrammed to ask for a feedback, but it's better if you contact them personally right after they've received the product and for a review. **FeedbackFive** is a site that customizes your emails with feedback plea. One way to be ahead of the competition is actually using the technique of sending a "free" sample of your product to people who has bought your products before. Most of the time, free samples would attract more customers to buy other variations of your product. If not, hopefully they would send a good review for your offer. However, other times they would get your free sample without the promise of a single review. In cases like this, don't fret. That's the risk you have to be willing to make, this really would show how important positive reviews really are in the long run. Some people shy away from this method because it would cost them a lot of time, effort, and money to secure at least one review with a percentage of getting nothing in return. In the long run, it will prove beneficial for you. With reviews reaching far back a couple of years and recent reviews, they would show consistency and reliability in the eyes of the customers.

FeedbackFive website: http://www.feedbackfive.com/

YouTube Video Tutorials
- **FeedbackFive "Email Campaigns" Introduction:** https://goo.gl/6w9Vsa
- **Amazon Product Review Software: FeedbackFive:** https://goo.gl/MSyrHA

- **Amazon Seller Suspension & Prevention: Tips for Avoidance:** https://goo.gl/UN767x

b. How To Deal With Negative Reviews?

If you are one who takes criticism to heart too deeply, you might want to find means to calm down and meditate. Often, people are so engrossed with their ratings and have become paranoid with any negative reviews that they lash out when there's a slight tone of criticism. Don't do that. You may also feel that your product has no faults, and you have the persuading power to show the Amazon personnel that their bad review is unreasonable. Don't do that either. Better yet, the best thing to do is to not do anything at all. The thing with reviews is that it's their personal opinion. Not everyone will like what you're selling. Heck, your service could be top notch with glitter and gold packaging and you still will have a bad review just because of the item and not your service. Bestseller items being sold millions of times over will still have thousands of poor reviews. Your aim is to envelop those bad reviews with awesome reviews tenfold.

When you are blasted by negative reviews, do not come across as defensive and reply to their comments. You will put yourself in their mindset allowing you to fight back and that will always end up with a loss. Most of the time, they're just being comical and probably have nothing better to do.

One way to address this is to communicate in a medium that involves only two parties: you and the bad review. You address this problem privately and ask with utmost sincerity for them to remove it by explaining your side. But if they still won't budge, leave it be. When can you reply to a review? You can out in the open reply with a soft greeting and thanks when they've posted favorable opinions. But even then, it's tricky. When your product is selling at a rapid rate, you can't say thank you to each comment. You'll be wasting your time. If you only reply to a few comments and not the rest, it would show preference to people and others would feel left out.

You shouldn't create false accounts to cover up the negative comments with 5-star praises. You shouldn't even do it yourself. If your product were great and your service outstanding, you would feel more accomplished hearing about it from other people. Amazon has a way of detecting fake reviews and it would look desperate. It will come back and bite you in the rear end with forgery being a sin in the Amazon world. You won't be praised and respected. If you're cheating people to get customers, there's a chance you'll cheat people of their money. Not a good reputation.

There may be times where Amazon will aid you in removing a comment, but not because it has something bad to say about your product. Routinely, Amazon does not tolerate comments that have nothing to do with the products entirely. Most of the time, comments come in the form of links to separate websites, advertising of some sort or random and obscene language and images. Amazon is trying to create a healthy environment of product discourse and not a spam war.

c. Benefits Of Amazon Reviews

There are plenty of repercussions of having an Amazon review and even more rewarding if they're positive. What easier way to get your product out in the open to a large market when your customers are the ones advertising it for you. With one faithful and enthusiastic customer, you can expect to see a ripple effect of interested buyers. People like being taken care of with the first-class service. Paying attention to the tiny details is already a huge thing for them. Even if a customer has received the wrong product, going up and beyond to make sure they get the item they paid for and adding extra incentives will be the best thing to do.

Amazon's top reviewers are primarily the celebrities in the Amazon scene. Everyone wants to be their friends, give them a free sample and are surprisingly feared. Some top Amazon reviewers are using the profession of providing quality reviews to people's products as their living. What happens is that a supplier would give free samples for them to try out and give a feedback. Since consumers adore social proofs and opinions from this group of people and have already established a following, one positive review of a product will lead to the profit and purchase rate skyrocketing.

To track down top reviewers, Amazon has compiled a list of their top customer reviewers for people to reach them. They are divided into their category of specialization. You can get their information by hovering your mouse over their names and clicking on the link leading to their profile page.

You'll need to convince them to review your product by explaining you're the rationale of your item. Next you'll need to send them your product for free and be patient with the review. Note that there's no guarantee if the review they'll reply with is positive or negative. It's a huge risk you'll have to take if you actually want to improve. If you're confident with your product, go ahead and try it out. If you're not, find ways to improve and alter your product before asking for a review. To minimize the risk, make sure the reviewer's interests is within your product's subcategory. Otherwise, they would be making a review for something they know nothing about and most likely dislike to begin with. Also, emphasize that they're not required to send a reply. Making the conversation by email as personal and tight as possible would make them feel more comfortable. They get plenty of people asking for help; you'll need to stand out from the crowd. Half the time your request will be ignored and it gives you other options to find other reviewers and try the process again. When you receive a great review, don't forget to thank the Amazon top reviewer for their time and effort. They probably have a huge network of other top reviewers so you should take that as an advantage by keeping them close through special promotions and discount coupons for their next purchase with you.

YouTube Video Tutorial
- **Product Reviews: Product Launch Promotion Strategies for Amazon FBA:** https://goo.gl/kr2UPD
- **Launching First Amazon Product + Unique Review Strategy:** https://goo.gl/bmfYnD
- **How To Get More Reviews and More Conversions : for Your Amazon FBA Product :** https://goo.gl/veB8QA

CHAPTER 13: BECOMING A TOP SELLER IN AMAZON

As we've been discussing in this book. FBA is the best way to sell online. They will take the products you are going to sell, store, and ship it for you. You will not have to deal with any type of customer service either since they will handle all returns and exchanges. We've gone over the benefits of selling through Amazon using FBA and now we'll discuss strategies to become a top seller.

There's no guarantee that you will sell your products and make money automatically. This is why we'll need to have launch strategies that will put our products at the top of rankings when customers search for products.

To summarize, the Amazon algorithm for ranking products is, the more sales and good reviews the products has then the higher its ranking will be on Amazon. A highly ranked product gets a lot of sales without the seller doing any work.

Giving away products is a great way to garner sales and positive reviews. Since customers are always looking for deals online make sure you set a very low price ($1-2) to get buyers' attention. This is a great way to rank up the list quickly. Amazon even has a function where you can set up promotions for a product and print out **coupon claim codes**. Give these coupons to your friends and family, have them order the product at a low price using the coupon and then ask them for their honest reviews.

Creating a Promotion page: http://goo.gl/pzFyzB

The downside to this strategy is that it will be nearly impossible to make any profit. You may get as close to breaking even but that is only if your product is cheap to make. Therefore, I recommend starting with an inexpensive product first so you don't lose as much money while ranking up the lists.

Amazon Ads is the advertising feature on Amazon that allows sellers to get exposure for the products on the website. I recommend that every seller should be using Amazon Ads because it will lead to more sales, which will also rank your product higher. When first beginning with Amazon Ads we should start with the "Automatic" targeting system. This way you're ads will be spread around the website evenly. There's also a "Daily Budget" that is set to determine how much exposure your product receives.

The higher the budget, the more advertisement you get for your product.

Once your product begins selling, head to the report section in Amazon Ads and search what keywords buyers are using when they search for your product. After identifying the words switch the targeting to "Manual" and enter those specific keywords.

There are certain websites designed for Amazon sellers that promote and sell your products on other people's list. This will spread your product to other online markets and gain even more exposure. There are fees however and usually, you will have to give away your product with coupons. This is not necessary but for many products they do help boost sales and reviews. I recommend websites such as **Buview** or **Zonblast**.

Buview website: https://buview.com/
Zonblast website: https://www.zonblast.com/

There are bloggers from all around the world who's hobby is to receive products, review them and if they enjoyed the item then they will happily advertise it on their Blog and share it with other bloggers. A popular website for this is **Tomoson.com**. All you have to do is set up an account for free and list your product. Bloggers will come flocking wanting to receive and promote your product.

Tomoson website: https://www.tomoson.com/

As a requirement, you need to give away your product using $1 coupons. Once a member from Tomoson receives the product you have the option to have them either post a review on their Blog and then link to Amazon, put together a Youtube video review then linking it to Amazon, post it on their social media with a link to Amazon or to just leave an honest review on Amazon.

Most of the time this service is free but many popular Bloggers will charge you for this type of advertisement. The range could be from $10 all the way to $50. However, if the Blogger is popular enough with many followers then spending this extra money can generate a lot of sales.

The key to becoming a top seller is not maximizing profit at first but to generate sales and good reviews. Giving your products away using Amazon coupons to people who will generate good reviews for your products does this. Once our item is high in the rankings then it will sell on its own.

One of the easiest ways to sell more on Amazon is to raise the ranking of your products. This has a lot of advantages and will increase your sales dramatically, but the most important thing is that you don't have to do anything. If the ranking of your product increases then it will appear higher and have a lot of visibility, which will lead to a lot of new sales without needing you to change anything about the product.

CONCLUSION

So, now you have been given the ultimate guide into the virtual world of Amazon FBA, as well as included steps on what you should do and tips that you can follow in order to obtain a successful online business.

What more can you ask for?

For those of you who have an already established online business or who are planning to start up an online business, just wait and see how much the given information provided to you from this book will boost up your sales. This in-depth guide will skyrocket you into becoming the next top-of-the-line online seller in your market.

You have been blessed with the knowledge that many of your competitor's may not know, so be sure to take note and study carefully the techniques that you can use for your online business in the future.

Use this not just as a step-by-step guide, but also as your online marketing bible because when you do, your business may almost be guaranteed its success.

What are you waiting for? Go get rich! Be a millionaire!

Made in the USA
Middletown, DE
11 October 2017